WHAT ABOUT MURDER?

A Guide to Books About Mystery and Detective Fiction

by
JON L. BREEN

The Scarecrow Press, Inc.
Metuchen, N.J., & London 1981

Library of Congress Cataloging in Publication Data

Breen, Jon L., 1943-
  What about murder?

  Includes index.
  1. Detective and mystery stories--History and
criticism--Bibliography. 2. Detective and mystery
stories--Technique--Bibliography. I. Title.
Z5917.D5B73 [PN3448.D4]   016.823'0872   81-645
ISBN 0-8108-1413-7   AACR2

†

†

For Rita

... who knows where the
bodies are buried.

† TABLE OF CONTENTS

†

Dear Reader:

Sometime in 1940, D. Appleton-Century Company mailed us the galley proofs of Howard Haycraft's <u>Murder for Pleasure: The Life and Times of the Detective Story</u>. We read the book with so much pleasure that we sent the following comment to the publisher: "We were so completely fascinated by Mr. Haycraft's <u>Murder for Pleasure</u> that we read clear through the book in one sitting. It is a landmark in the history of detective fiction--a brilliant, necessary, long-overdue study, written with charm and authority."

In the forty years since, only a few nonfiction books dealing with the mystery genre have evoked a similar response in me. But now I can write almost the same testimonial for Mr. Breen's book. "I became so fascinated by Mr. Breen's title that once I started reading it, I put aside my own urgent deadlines. It is a landmark in the field of books about mysteries--a brilliant, necessary, long-overdue reference work, written with charm and authority."

After all these years, more than fifty, as a player in "the grandest game in the world" (John Dickson Carr's phrase), I still find the roll call of names--of authors, titles, detectives, critics, historians, biographers, bibliographers, publishers, collectors, fans, and aficionados--I still hear their sounds as a musical and mystical incantation. If your heart belongs to mysteries, the magical names in this book will cast their spell over you too.   †

Ellery Queen

After a boyhood in which Mr. Keen, Tracer of Lost Persons,
Hearthstone of the Death Squad, Mr. Chameleon, the Hardy
Boys, the cinematic Charlie Chan, and Djuna (of the Ellery
Queen, Jr., books) loomed uncommonly large, I became a
reader and collector of adult detective fiction in 1956.   In
that year, I bought my first issue of Ellery Queen's Mystery
Magazine, read a novel called The Frightened Stiff, by Kelley Roos, and headed resolutely down a path of crime from
which there has been no turning back.
        Almost immediately, I decided that reading mysteries
was not enough.   I wanted to read about mysteries--their
history and technique, the lives of their authors.   And I
wanted to compare my opinions with those of other readers.
It didn't take long to learn what was available in the way of
writing about mystery and detective fiction, because there
wasn't much.
        I combed old issues of EQMM for the extensive and
informative introductions to individual stories.   I learned
that Howard Haycraft (whose "Speaking of Crime" column in
EQMM of the forties was a prime source of news and opinion, albeit a few years old) had written the definitive history
of the form in Murder for Pleasure, and I managed to find
a copy of that.   I learned that Anthony Boucher of the New
York Times and James Sandoe of the Herald-Tribune were
the best reviewers going, and I eagerly sought their columns.
Book Review Digest proved a reliable source for locating
mystery reviews.   (Alas, it isn't any more.)   Certain older
titles of criticism and history, like H. Douglas Thomson's
Masters of Mystery, proved difficult to track down, though
I finally did.   I learned that some of the best surveys of de-

tective fiction appeared in old anthology introductions by editors like Dorothy L. Sayers, Willard Huntington Wright, E. M. Wrong, and Ronald A. Knox, and of course I sought out Haycraft's anthology of essays, The Art of the Mystery Story, and Queen's full-scale bibliography of books of detective short stories.

As for biographical information, some of the best-known writers turned up in Twentieth Century Authors (another Haycraft project, in collaboration with Stanley Kunitz), and a very few were eminent enough to have book-length biographies or autobiographies. For most, though, there was nothing to be found. There were a few scattered how-to manuals and of course several volumes of Sherlockiana, but that was about it. Any new study of the field was cause for celebration.

Now times have changed with a vengeance. The year that marked the turning point was 1967, when Allen J. Hubin founded The Armchair Detective, a rallying point for communicative fans who could now learn of each other's existence and exchange views. Two other fanzines, Len and June Moffatt's John D. MacDonald Bibliophile and Lianne Carlin's The Mystery Lover's (later Reader's) Newsletter, began at about the same time, but the birth of TAD as much as anything brought about the flood of mystery-fiction studies of the seventies.

In the past few years, biographical, bibliographical, critical, encyclopedic, and ephemeral books about mystery-crime-detective-espionage fiction have poured forth in profusion. Where once the Mystery Writers of America would give a special Edgar award to a work about the genre when a good one happened to turn up, in the years since 1976 the biographical-critical award has become a regular category.

On an admittedly smaller scale, the flood of mystery analyses parallels the rise of film books. Where once any new book about the movies would be eagerly scooped up by buffs, now they are published in such numbers, and with such a wide range in quality, originality, and seriousness, that the buff must pick and choose. As whole volumes have been devoted to guiding the student of film through all the book-length sources available, it is now time for a guidebook to do the same thing for students and readers of mystery fiction.

While this is a bibliography, and as complete as the compiler can make it in point of titles covered, its main purpose is to evaluate tht titles listed, to try to give the reader some idea not just of what the books are and do but of which ones are worth reading, which are to be avoided, and where the others fall in the vast area in between.

The initial intent was to include every monograph ever published about mystery and detective fiction. Cut-and-dried as that may sound, there were still decisions to be made about what should and should not be included. It became necessary to eliminate certain categories of material, usually to avoid duplicating the efforts of others and to keep the work from becoming unwieldy. The following are some of the questionable categories and the decisions made on them:

1) <u>Sherlock Holmes.</u> The most immediate decision to omit involved this famous character and his creator (or, if you prefer, his biographer's literary agent), Sir Arthur Conan Doyle. Though they are both referred to frequently in many (perhaps most) of the general books listed here, all of the books dealing with them solely have been omitted. There are so many such titles, they would probably take up over half the bibliography if they were to be included, and they have been more than adequately covered elsewhere. As

a guide to the literature of Sherlock Holmes, I strongly
recommend two volumes, both the work of Ronald Burt De
Waal: The World Bibliography of Sherlock Holmes and Dr.
Watson: A Classified and Annotated List of Materials Re-
lating to Their Lives and Adventures. Boston: New York
Graphic Society, 1974. xiv, 526p.; and The International
Sherlock Holmes. Hamden, Connecticut: Archon Books,
1980. 621p.

2) Motion pictures. A few books specifically devoted to film detectives and spies have been included, as
have books about screen adaptations of individual mystery
writers. However, books on gangster films, film noir, and
individual directors of suspense films (Alfred Hitchcock, for
example) have been omitted.

3) Dealer and exhibition catalogues. Though many
of these contain useful information, they have been omitted
from the listing because they are seldom readily available;
they are tied to a particular time or event for their primary
usefulness, and there are too many of them to cover with
any degree of comprehensiveness.

4) Publicity materials. Pamphlets issued by publishers to honor or publicize their authors have for the most
part been omitted, except when they have some special bibliographic or reference value. The reasons for omission
are generally the same as for dealer and exhibition catalogues.

5) Works on individual authors. Works about individual authors primarily known as mystery writers have been
included, even in cases where genre-related content is relatively small. However, writers who have made a significant
contribution to literature outside the mystery field have generally been excluded, especially when they have been extensively written about in monographs. Writers in this category

include Edgar Allan Poe, Charles Dickens, Graham Greene, Ronald A. Knox, C. Day Lewis (Nicholas Blake), Isaac Asimov, G. K. Chesterton, G. D. H. Cole, Eden Phillpotts, C. P. Snow, Vincent Starrett, and Rupert Croft-Cooke (Leo Bruce). The reasons for their exclusion are basically the same as for Holmes and Doyle. (And, as with Holmes and Conan Doyle, they are covered in many of the general works listed.)

6) Volumes of mixed subjects. As a general rule, the books that have been listed deal exclusively with mystery and detective fiction or with a writer primarily known for work in the genre. In some instances, however, collections of essays have been included that also deal with other subjects but include more than one essay concerning the mystery field. In addition, a few books dealing with popular fiction generally have been included if their mystery content is of interest. In these cases, the extent of genre-related material has been clearly indicated.

7) Foreign-language works. Volumes in languages other than English have been excluded. However, a partial exception has been made for two Swedish titles with some English-language content and bibliographic data useful to English readers.

Within the guidelines above, the goal has been to list and comment upon every book in English about the mystery-detective field. I have attempted to examine every title listed and (except for a few cases in Part VII) have succeeded. The few items not examined are indicated as such in the entry.

Each entry lists first English-language edition, first American edition if different, and significantly revised editions. Reprints are not included. The entry includes the

following information: author, title, others named on the
title page (e. g. , illustrator, translator, introduction-writer,
editor), series (if any), place, publisher, date, pagination,
and the presence of any of the following special features:
illustrations (illus.), bibliography (bibl.), index. In cases
where the whole book is clearly by its title a bibliography or
an index, these designations have been omitted as redundant.
The term "bibliography" is generally used in the loose sense
of any listing of books and other printed sources. Fully descriptive bibliographies are indicated as such in the annotation.

The listing is divided into seven parts:

Part I. GENERAL HISTORIES. (Works devoted to a
historical overview of the mystery genre, usually concentrating on the detective story.)

Part II. REFERENCE BOOKS. (Encyclopedias, dic-
tionaries, bibliographies, and other items that by their format and content seem likelier candidates for the reference
shelves of most libraries than the circulating shelves. Reference books on individual authors are included in Part VII.)

Part III. SPECIAL SUBJECTS. (Works concerning
particular aspects, theories, or subgroupings of the crime-
mystery-detective genre.)

Part IV. COLLECTED ESSAYS AND REVIEWS.
(Compilations of individual pieces by single authors or various authors.)

Part V. TECHNICAL MANUALS. (Devoted to instructing the prospective writer in the genre.)

Part VI. COFFEE-TABLE BOOKS. (Not a pejora-
tive comment on the quality of the contents but rather a
classification according to format. All the books in this section have a larger-than-average page size and are profusely

illustrated, though the text may vary from meaty to virtually absent.)

Part VII. WORKS ON INDIVIDUAL AUTHORS. (Biographical, autobiographical, critical, and bibliographical works on writers primarily known for mystery and detective fiction.)

†

This is a personal reference book, and, as I point out more than once in the pages that follow, personal reference books tend to idiosyncratic, provocative, and sometimes infuriating. The opinions here are mine and will probably provoke some disagreement. (Indeed, I'll be disappointed if they don't.) I believe that writing about entertainment should itself be entertaining, and I thus get impatient with academic studies that are pretentious and a chore to read. But I also get impatient with fannish writings that are strictly antiquarian without any real point to make. Those few books that strike a perfect balance between the academic and the fannish seem to me the best, and my annotations will make it clear which those are.

The decision of what to include and what to exclude is also mine, and some will no doubt quarrel with my choices. Others may find I have left out titles that clearly qualify for inclusion simply because I didn't know about them. I hope readers will let me know of any such lapses for inclusion in a possible supplement or revised edition, which may or may not come to pass some few years hence.

There is no reason to think that the flow of books about the mystery field will stop in the foreseeable future. Many tantalizing volumes are in the works at the moment, and perusal of this book will point up many areas where book-length studies are lacking and needed.

For example, with all the books coming out about Agatha Christie and Dorothy L. Sayers, there is only one full-length book about Ellery Queen and only a thin pamphlet each about S. S. Van Dine and John Dickson Carr. Raymond Chandler and Dashiell Hammett have been widely written about, but there is no book at all on Cornell Woolrich. For all the studies and biographies of Ian Fleming, there is no book on the fad author of a decade earlier, Mickey Spillane, and (more regrettably) no book on John Le Carré, Eric Ambler, or Len Deighton. And how many authors, even those about whom several volumes have been written, have been the subject of a critical guide of the caliber of Francis M. Nevins, Jr. 's Royal Bloodline, on Queen, or Robert Barnard's A Talent to Deceive, on Christie?

More generally, we have had no history to date of the police procedural novel, a fascinating field for exploration. And, surprisingly, there is not any book-length study of the private-eye novel that does not a) have a special thematic ax to grind or b) limit itself to a very small number of authors. There is much new ground to cover, and mystery fans should look forward to what the next few years will bring.

An original intention of this work was to include listings of all the periodicals devoted to criticism and appreciation of the form. The same factors that make these journals a serials librarian's nightmare--irregular publication schedules, frequent changes of address and format, and short life-spans--also discouraged me from trying to cover them comprehensively. However, I will list a few fanzines and semi-pro periodicals that have kept to at least a fairly regular publication schedule and have included some excellent articles, checklists, reviews, and (sometimes best of all) letters to the editor.

The Armchair Detective. Quarterly. Edited by
Michael Seidman, who recently replaced founder Allen J. Hubin in that capacity. Published by The Mysterious Press,
129 West 56th Street, New York, NY 10019.

The Mystery FANcier. Bimonthly. Edited and published by Guy M. Townsend, 840 E. Main St. , #5, Blytheville,
AR 72315.

The Poisoned Pen. Bimonthly. Edited and published
by Jeffrey Meyerson, 50 1st Place, Brooklyn, NY 11231.

A newer publication with a professional glossiness but
(thus far) less impressive articles than its amateur brethren
is Mystery. Bimonthly. Edited and published by Stephen L.
Smoke, 304 South Broadway, Suite 202, Los Angeles, CA
90013.

Since subscription prices are subject to sudden change,
I have not attempted to list them.

† ACKNOWLEDGMENTS

Many institutions and individuals contributed (directly or indirectly, knowingly or unknowingly) to the writing of this
book. I particularly want to thank my colleagues at Rio
Hondo College Library, especially Steve Brown (indefatigable
pursuer of interlibrary loans) and Fern Gagné (who helped
me raid the memory banks of OCLC). I also owe a debt to
the staffs of the British Library; the public libraries of Los
Angeles, Huntington Beach, and Fountain Valley, California,
and of Doncaster, South Yorkshire, England, and St. Andrew's,

Scotland; and the research collections of UCLA and California State University, Fullerton. Francis M. Nevins, Jr., and Julia and Tim Johnson offered valuable suggestions at various stages of the project.

Bibliographers whose earlier efforts in this field made the ground easier to dig include Enola Stewart, Robert E. Briney, and the team of Tage la Cour and Harald Mogensen. The scholars and historians whose pioneering efforts made a book like this possible are too numerous to mention, but three stand out: Howard Haycraft, Ellery Queen (Frederic Dannay), and Allen J. Hubin.

Above all, thanks are due my wife, Rita, who compiled the index, proofread the manuscript, and encouraged the whole project from the beginning.   †

WHAT
ABOUT
MURDER?
†

1. Haycraft, Howard. <u>Murder for Pleasure: The Life and</u>
<u>Times of the Detective Story.</u> New York: Appleton-Century,
1941. xviii, 409p. Illus. , bibl. , index.

Though Haycraft's history becomes the first entry in
this book through a combination of organizational and alphabetical accident, its primacy is entirely appropriate. For
many years, it was the one authoritative source on the history of detective fiction, and forty years after its publication
it remains one of the best and most valuable works in the
field, beautifully written and boundlessly influential. One of
the book's chief attributes is its painstaking accuracy. Haycraft has rarely been impeached on factual grounds.
Very much a detective-story purist, Haycraft declares
most thrillers and spy novels out of bounds. He takes what
is now regarded as the conventional approach to the history
of the field, beginning with Edgar Allan Poe; discussing
Charles Dickens, Wilkie Collins, and Emile Gaboriau in a
transitional chapter; then devoting a full chapter to Sir Arthur Conan Doyle and Sherlock Holmes. He divides the period between the creation of Holmes and 1941 into three seg-
ments--The Romantic Era (1890-1914), The Golden Age (1918-
1930), and The Moderns (1930-)--and gives over a chapter
to each of these periods in England and America. He also
devotes a single chapter to the Continental Detective Story
since Gaboriau.
Subsequent chapters on the rules of detective-story
writing and on the writer's market (with some economic specifics that must have been discouraging to the aspiring mystery writer of 1941) take on the aspect of a how-to manual.
Haycraft also offers bibliographies of critical writings on the

genre and of detective-story "cornerstones," a quiz, and a who's-who listing of detectives and other continuing characters, identifying their creators.

It is interesting to speculate on how much Haycraft's judgments have molded opinion of later commentators. His denigration of Gaboriau may have scared off generations of potential readers of the French pioneer. Some recent commentators, notably R. F. Stewart (see #4) have done their best to rehabilitate the creator of Lecoq. In discussing Collins, he gives the impression that the author of The Moonstone wrote no other detective stories of note, another view being corrected by present-day critics. His devastating account of Fergus Hume's The Mystery of a Hansom Cab, though disputed by Julian Symons (see #5), has been taken as gospel by many writers on the form. He also pins an unjustified (in my opinion) charge of humorlessness on S. S. Van Dine.

Most of Haycraft's opinions, though, stand the test of time remarkably well. For all his formalist conservatism, he gives Dashiell Hammett his due as an important innovator, although Raymond Chandler (whose impact had yet to be fully felt) is not mentioned, except for an identification of Philip Marlowe in the who's-who section.

One final point: it is both fascinating and moving to see how the shadow of World War II permeates this book, written as Britain's horror was well underway but before the attack on Pearl Harbor had involved the United States in the war. There are sad references to the deaths in the Nazi air raids of Helen Simpson and A. G. Macdonell of London's Sherlock Holmes Society. We read of 79-year-old R. Austin Freeman continuing his writing in "a personally-designed bomb-shelter in his garden" (page 69). In a footnote (pages 203-204), John Dickson Carr describes with irrepressible humor his brushes with death and the destruction of his furniture in three separate Blitzkrieg attacks. Haycraft charges Americans with the responsibility of keeping the form alive while their British colleagues are otherwise engaged. One wonders how much the existence of Murder for Pleasure can be attributed to the therapeutic value of clinging to this symbol of an orderly society as the shadow of war spread across the globe.

2.   Murch, A. E.   The Development of the Detective Novel. London: Peter Owen, 1958.   272p.   Illus., bibl., index. American edition, New York: Philosophical Library, 1958. 272p.   Illus., bibl., index.

Murch perceived a gap in previous studies of the form in their coverage of the early history of detective fiction. Thus, she discusses in some detail the contributions of Ann Radcliffe, William Godwin, Charles Brockden Brown, Bulwer-Lytton, James Fenimore Cooper, Vidocq, and Balzac, not even reaching Poe until page 67. Covering much material not discussed elsewhere, this is basically a worthy book, but Murch makes the mistake of also trying to cover the twentieth century briefly. Possibly relying too much on secondary sources, including Sutherland Scott (I would guess; see #3), she commits many errors and thus casts doubt on the accuracy of her account of the earlier period.

This volume drew one of the most damning reviews ever written by the generally kindhearted critic Anthony Boucher. In the New York Times Book Review (December 14, 1958, page 20), Boucher wrote, "Throughout Mrs. Murch gets names and dates wrong, describes short stories as novels and serious tales as humorous, and in short displays no evidence of having read what she's writing about." The novel/short-story confusion may stem from Murch's habit of putting both kinds of titles in italics, rather than quoting short-story titles. Thus, one could easily be mislead that Dickens's "Hunted Down" was a novel, though Murch doesn't explicitly say so. This is not so much misidentification as a failure to differentiate. The fact remains, though, that Murch is often either vague or inaccurate on authors, titles, dates, and series. The nearer she approaches the present, the less useful her work becomes.

3. Scott, Sutherland. Blood in Their Ink: The March of the Modern Mystery Novel. Foreword by A. Beverley Baxter. London: Stanley Paul, 1953. 200p. Index.

To Scott, mystery equals detective, and he is an extreme traditionalist, objecting to strong love interest or humor and very wary of sex. The obvious sincerity and enthusiasm of his book will win over many readers by the end, though it presents a broad target for any commentator in a sour mood: disorganized to the point of free-association, rather ineptly written, repetitious, full of doubtful generalizations and vacuous remarks. Part history and part technical manual, it ultimately seems to fall in the first category, though paradoxically most of its more valuable comments fall in the second. The main focus of attention is on the post-World War I detective novel.

An interesting section discusses the artificial elaborations of the detective novel in the thirties: footnotes, diagrams, maps, character lists, epigraphs, title patterns, clue-finders, and so forth. Scott claims to deplore these accoutrements, though he admits to using them in some of his own novels. He also offers an entertaining chapter on titles.

Some of Scott's preferences among mystery writers are rather eccentric compared with those of other commentators. He finds many writers worthy of note who have been ignored in most other works on the field: Brian Flynn, Christopher Bush, Harry Stephen Keeler (he calls The Amazing Web "a truly great mystery story" on page 63), Douglas K. Browne, Todd Downing, Milton M. Propper, Robert J. Casey, Charlotte Murray Russell, Margaret Erskine, Thurman Warriner, Bruce Hamilton, William Wiegand, Sam S. Taylor. The usually neglected Leonard Gribble is constantly turning up on the rolls of the great in this volume.

For all its errors (such as consistent references to S. S. "Van Dyne") and idiosyncrasies, this is a hard book not to like, mainly because Scott comes across as such a humorous, self-effacing fellow. " ... I recall the reviewer who stated that my first novel resembled Hamlet inasmuch as there were seven corpses. Unfortunately, that was all he said" (page 136).

4. Stewart, R. F. ... And Always a Detective: Chapters on the History of Detective Fiction. Newton Abbot, England: David and Charles, 1980. 351p. Bibl. , index.

Stewart's subtitle is well chosen, for this is not so much a straightforward history of the form as a learned nibbling around the edges. The initial discussion of the definition and etymology of "detective story" may strike some readers as hair-splitting or angels-on-the-head-of-a-pin arguing. In the early chapters, Stewart tries to reach some kind of synthesis of Murch (see #2), Haycraft (see #1), Symons (see #5), Régis Messac (whose 1929 study, "Detective Novel" et l'Influence de la Pensée Scientifique, appears only in French), and other previous historians. This is decidedly not the history of the form one should come to first.

Stewart parallels nineteenth-century "sensation fiction" with twentieth-century detective fiction very convincingly. He delights in quoting hundred-year-old critical comments that sound as if they could have been written much later. He offers interesting material on real-life detectives of the last century and on early detective writers like Waters and James

McGovan, pointing out how rudimentary their accounts of
police work were and how little influence they had in the
development of the classical detective story originated by
Poe.

Stewart spends more space in appreciation of Gaboriau than any other of the genre's historians (at least in English). Conan Doyle's large debt to Gaboriau is definitively
pinned down in a series of parallel passages from L'Affaire
Lerouge and A Study in Scarlet. The spirited defense of
Lecoq's creator, as much as anything, makes this well-
written volume, scholarly without being boring, a candidate
for the permanent shelf.

An appendix presents notes, corrections, and comments on Dorothy Glover and Graham Greene's Victorian
Detective Fiction (see #14), mainly disagreements as to who
is the detective in the works listed.

5. Symons, Julian. Bloody Murder: From the Detective
Story to the Crime Novel. London: Faber and Faber, 1972.
254p. Index. American title: Mortal Consequences: A
History--From the Detective Story to the Crime Novel.
New York: Harper and Row, 1972. x, 269p. Index.

This is the first major history of the detective story
since Haycraft's Murder for Pleasure (see #1), which it
supplements but in no sense replaces. As the subtitle suggests, Symons's main theme is the gradual development of
the detective story away from the formal puzzle into the
wider category of crime novel, closer (via its increased
realism, depth of character and theme, and social observation) to mainstream literature. Thus, Symons values trends
that Haycraft, along with Jacques Barzun and Wendell Hertig
Taylor and other purists, dreaded.

Following an opening chapter analyzing the appeal of
crime and suspense fiction (and basically rejecting the idea
of categorization), Symons launches on a chronological history. He pays more attention to pre-Poe detection than did
Haycraft, spending more time on Vidocq and discussing William Godwin's Caleb Williams, not mentioned by Haycraft.
He devotes most of the space between Poe and Doyle to the
usual trio of Dickens, Collins, and Gaboriau, but also brings
in Sheridan LeFanu and other writers on whom Haycraft is
silent. He also defends Fergus Hume's The Mystery of a
Hansom Cab against the brickbats generally accorded it.

In one rare instance of sloppy scholarship, Symons
ticks off the plots of some of his favorite short stories about

Jacques Futrelle's The Thinking Machine without naming them
so that the reader can look them up.

Offering fresh views of many often-discussed writers,
Symons values Mary Roberts Rinehart, Dorothy L. Sayers,
and H. C. Bailey less than most other commentators. But
he does have some kind words for a couple of American
writers who have recently been favorite whipping boys: S. S.
Van Dine (whose Philo Vance he compliments at the direct
expense of Lord Peter Wimsey) and Erle Stanley Gardner.
For all his celebration of the contemporary crime novel,
Symons is anything but contemptuous of many of the products
of the Golden Age.

Symons makes a good case for looking into a number
of writers generally neglected in other accounts: from the
early days, M. McDonnell Bodkin, and from more recent
times, John Franklin Bardin, Margot Bennett, John Bingham,
Shelley Smith, and Roy Fuller.

Though not making a rigid separation of British and
American product as Haycraft does, Symons generally discusses novels and short stories separately. He gives more
attention to the latter-day short than most commentators,
discussing such writers as Stanley Ellin and Roy Vickers and
saluting the importance of Ellery Queen's Mystery Magazine
is keeping the form alive.

After a chapter charting the differences between the
old detective story and the new crime novel (somewhat over-
simplified and always, of course, to the disadvantage of the
detective story) and discussing the police procedural, Symons
resorts to a catchall chapter, mentioning writers and topics
from various periods not yet dealt with. He then devotes a
chapter to the history of the spy story and another to his
predictions for the future of the crime novel in its different
guises.

The book is less error-free than Murder for Pleasure.
It mistakenly states that the Ellery Queen team wrote under
the name Drury Lane (Lane was the detective, Barnaby Ross
the pseudonym); dates Rex Stout's birth as 1866 (an obvious
typo); and makes several errors in a brief paragraph about
the Patrick Quentin collaboration. But the howlers are far
less frequent than in most books about detective fiction up
to that time, and Symons's lucid, witty style and original
views make this one of the more valuable studies of the
genre.

6. Symons, Julian. The Detective Story in Britain (Writers
and Their Work, No. 145). London: Longmans, Green, for

the British Council and National Book League, 1962.   48p.
Bibl.

    This pamphlet, a thirty-page essay with a twelve-
page checklist, is superseded by Bloody Murder (see #5
above) as a vehicle for Symons's ideas about the detective
story and its metamorphosis into the crime novel.   Some of
Symons's views seem more inflammatory in their compressed
form.   Points fully expressed in the later book-length history come out as unfairly sweeping generalizations here.
The tarring of the classical school is rather overdone--Van
Dine did not say that a detective novel should exclude all
characterization, and Ronald Knox surely did not lack wit
as Symons claims.   It is satisfying to be able to report that
some of the writers Symons pronounces forgotten and unread
as of 1962--Arthur Morrison, Baroness Orczy, Ernest Bramah, R. Austin Freeman--have since been reprinted and
rediscovered.

7.   Thomson, H. Douglas.   Masters of Mystery: A Study
of the Detective Story.   London: Collins, 1931.   288p.
Index.   American edition, with a new introduction and footnotes by E. F. Bleiler, New York: Dover, 1978.   288p.
Index.

    The pioneer history of the genre was pretty well
superseded by Haycraft (see #1) and has been the target of
many slighting references over the years, some invited by
its wretched title.   But Thomson is an entertaining, witty,
quotable writer and well worth reading in the context of his
times and biases.
    Following a survey chapter on the definition, rules,
readership, and appeal of detective fiction, Thomson devotes
a chapter to broadly outlining the history of the form.   He
then gets down to specifics in subsequent chapters on Poe,
the French detective story, Sherlock Holmes, the "domestic"
detective story (E. C. Bentley, Lynn Brock, Philip Mac-
Donald, A. A. Milne), the "realistic" detective story (R.
Austin Freeman, Freeman Wills Crofts), the "orthodox" detective story (Agatha Christie), the thriller (Edgar Wallace,
A. E. W. Mason, J. S. Fletcher), and what Thomson calls
Tried Favourties (not to be misread, as I always do, Tired
Favourites), including Ronald Knox, Victor L. Whitecurch,
J. J. Connington, G. D. H. and M. I. Cole, G. K. Chester-
ton, H. C. Bailey, and Dorothy L. Sayers.   Thomson does
generally well by his countrymen, particularly Crofts,
Christie, and Freeman, and on the French pioneers.

Finally, Thomson devotes a chapter to the American detective story, and it is here primarily that he gets himself in trouble with later commentators. The Americans after Poe get seventeen pages, compared with twenty for the French. Although Thomson gives Van Dine, Ellery Queen (then the author of only two novels!), and Frances Noyes Hart their due, he dismisses Hammett in three sentences, in the process misidentifying Red Harvest and The Dain Curse as Sam Spade novels. Melville Davisson Post, Earl Derr Biggers, and Mary Roberts Rinehart are left out completely, though less significant writers like Isabel Ostrander and Hulbert Footner are discussed. He is unfair to Arthur B. Reeve by basing his discussion on the novelization of a silent movie serial (The Exploits of Elaine) rather than on the author's genuine detective stories. (This is roughly comparable to judging John D. MacDonald on the basis of I Could Go On Singing or Ellery Queen on The Penthouse Mystery.) Thomson's discussions deal almost entirely with the stories themselves, making no effort to place them in a biographical or historical context, as Haycraft does. Also, generally unlike Haycraft, Thomson has no compunctions about revealing the solutions of the stories he discusses.

The American edition, with Bleiler's introduction and notes, corrects some of the mistakes in the original edition, but not (curiously) a reference to the "Bond Street runners."

†

8.   Adey, Robert C. S.   Locked Rooms and Other Impossible Crimes.   London: Ferret Fantasy, 1979.   190p.

    Almost from the beginning, the seemingly impossible murder or theft has been a popular gimmick of writers of detective fiction, some of whom (notably John Dickson Carr and Clayton Rawson) have made it a virtually indispensable feature of their works.   Adey's bibliography is the first attempt to make a comprehensive list of all novels and short stories to set such problems.   Though admittedly incomplete, the list is of inestimable value to devotees.
    Following a brief nineteen-page history of locked-room/impossible-crime stories, Adey presents a numbered list, alphabetical by author, of 1,280 novels and stories involving such phenomena or (usually through a misleading title or an inaccurate blurb) seeming to.   Adey identifies series characters involved, if any, and includes a short phrase setting out the impossible problem involved, for example, "Death by stabbing in a voting booth under constant observation" (Edward D. Hoch's "The Problem of the Voting Booth") or "Disappearance of a horse from a locked and moving horsebox" (Michael Innes's "A Derby Horse").   The last section gives the solutions, a practice usually and quite rightly frowned upon but acceptable here since the book's arrangement makes it virtually impossible to stumble on one by accident.
    In this concluding section, Adey makes most of his critical comments on the stories, some quite funny.   Reading through the solutions without reference to the problems can be an enjoyable pastime.   Some examples at random:

"The victims were strangled by a hybrid creeper." "The child was picked up by an orang-utan." "The killer wore stilts." "The victim had been shot there by a circus cannon." "The murderer wore a tartan kilt and blended in with the scenery." In the solution appendix, Adey identifies Carter Dickson's (John Dickson Carr's) The Judas Window as "probably the best locked room mystery ever written" (page 151).

9.   Barnes, Melvyn.   Best Detective Fiction.   London: Clive Bingley, 1975.   121p.   American edition, Hamden, Connecticut: Linnet, 1975.   121p.

Barnes's annotated bibliography of highspots in the genre is arranged topically/chronologically and presented in a narrative format similar to Queen's Quorum (see #27). A checklist by author is included, but there is no title index. Criteria for inclusion are "excellence of plot, writing and/ or characterization, or a degree of innovation which has established or enhanced a trend" (page 7).   Spy stories and thrillers have been excluded.   Barnes lists the first English-language edition of the works included plus the first British edition if different.
Though it is an admittedly personal selection, reflecting the tastes and biases of the compiler, the writers included will raise few eyebrows.   Among the frequently overlooked writers Barnes champions are John Wainwright, Harry Carmichael, and Jeffrey Ashford.   It is very difficult to catch Barnes with an omission within his guidelines, though the absence of Helen McCloy and P. D. James is somewhat surprising.   On the whole, this is a sound and unexciting guidebook, with few errors but few sensations.

10.   Barzun, Jacques, and Wendell Hertig Taylor.   A Catalogue of Crime.   New York: Harper and Row, 1971.   xxxi, 831p.   Index.

This controversial volume is without question the most extensive annotated bibliography of detective fiction ever published.   It consists of an introduction and a six-part listing of 3,476 numbered entries, superbly indexed and cross-referenced.   The longest (2,304 entries) and most valuable section covers novels of detection, crime, mystery, and espionage.   The other five parts cover (more briefly) short stories, studies and histories, true crime, the literature of

Sherlock Holmes, and ghost stories. The two collaborators,
boyhood friends, had been exchanging information on detective
fiction for fifty years. Their witty and informative annotations are especially lively when the pair disagree. (On the
whole, WHT seems even harder to please than JB.) Brief
biographical sketches of some of the authors are included.

When Ordean Hagen's Who Done It? (see #16) made
its appearance, the most devastating review came from Barzun, writing in the American Scholar, who excoriated the
work for its errors and omissions. One could easily be
just as devastating on Barzun-Taylor as Barzun was on Hagen.
Errors of fact and eccentricities of inclusion and exclusion
abound.

The main criticism to be made is not that B and T
favor the classic puzzle over other departments of the mystery genre--they admit this bias from the start--nor is it
the lack of comprehensiveness, for they never claim to be
comprehensive. It is not even the large number of errors-
that-should-have-been-caught (for example, that Jack Vance
is a pseudonym of Henry Kuttner, that Maurice Leblanc died
in 1925, that Matt Helm and Scott Jordan are private eyes)
--at least a few such are inevitable in a project of this
magnitude. No, the big unanswered question is this: what
in the world were the criteria for inclusion? For a time,
I thought the duo had simply listed every detective story they
had ever read, but there is internal evidence that not even
this is the answer.

To be more specific: Why so many bad notices on
single short stories (see, for example, Edward D. Hoch,
Anthony Boucher, Vincent Cornier, and Erle Stanley Gardner
in Part 2), when so many good stories, by these writers
and others, are not mentioned at all? What is the function
of the "see also" references? In most cases, they do not
list all of the author's other works, so they must be in some
way selective. Surely they cannot be taken as recommended
reading when some of the annotated titles by the same authors
clearly are not recommended. Why relegate Helen McCloy's
brilliant first novel, Dance of Death, to a see-also when
several of her lesser works are discussed in detail? In a
five-page list of entries on Rex Stout, a particular favorite
of the compilers, why make a see-also of Double for Death,
which Stout himself regarded as his best detective story?
Finally, why waste an annotation on an obscure book by
Miles Burton (Murder at the Moorings) merely to pronounce
it "Very poor!" or list volumes few have ever heard of,
such as Monte Barrett's Murder at Belle Camille or Walter
C. Brown's The Second Guess, merely to dismiss them as

virtually worthless?

Trying to discover a rationale for what is in this book and what is not will inevitably be an unrewarding experience. It should be stressed that, for all its unevenness and idiosyncrasies, this is an important reference work that will not soon be equaled in the mystery field. Its greatest value is in its encouragement to readers to discover some lesser-known but worthy authors, including some British practitioners who have never been published in the United States.

In recent years, Barzun and Taylor have been contributing additional notes on detective fiction to The Armchair Detective, leading one to hope for either an expanded edition of A Catalogue of Crime or a supplementary volume. Either would be most welcome.

11. Breen, Jon L. The Girl in the Pictorial Wrapper. Rita A. Breen, Research Assistant. Carson: California State College, Dominguez Hills Library, 1972. 46p. Revised edition (Dominguez Hills Bibliographic Series, No. 2), Carson: California State College, Dominguez Hills Library, 1973. 50p.

Though paperback-original crime novels of the fifties and sixties seldom were reviewed, many of them got a hearing in Anthony Boucher's "Criminals at Large" column in the New York Times Book Review. But, for many years, these reviews were not indexed anywhere, either in Book Review Digest (which excluded paperbacks) or the Times's own index, which did not analyze the book review section consistently. To fill the gap, this pamphlet indexes all reviews of paperback originals in the column from 1953 to 1970, listing reviews by Boucher and his successor, Allen J. Hubin. Listing is by author with cross-references identifying pseudonyms. There is no title index.

The revised edition also includes reviews of paperback originals from "The Saint's Ratings," a column in The Saint Mystery Magazine from 1957 to 1959. The ratings given to the works reviewed (ranging from three haloes down to a pitchfork) are also included. The anonymous column was initially the work of Leslie Charteris but was usually written by Harry Harrison.

12. Clark, William J. An Author Index to Doc Savage Magazine. Los Angeles: M & B, 1971. 21p.

The index covers 181 issues of the famed hero pulp, 1933-1949. Stories are listed under the author's name in the order of their appearance, with the number of pages following the title. Pseudonyms and house names appear in italics, with the actual author's name given when known. Series characters are identified. Aside from Lester Dent, who wrote most of the Doc Savage novels under the byline Kenneth Robeson, some of the better-known contributors to the magazine included John D. MacDonald, Norman Daniels, Steve Fisher, and Jean Francis Webb. This is a valuable contribution to bibliographic control of the pulps.

13. Cook, Michael L. Murder by Mail: Inside the Mystery Book Clubs--With Complete Checklist. Evansville, Indiana: Cook, 1979. 109p. Index.

All selections of the three major mystery book clubs --the Detective Book Club, the Mystery Guild, and the short-lived Unicorn Mystery Book Club--are listed chronologically, with an index by author. A brief history of each club is included, with the information on the venerable Detective Book Club (established in 1942 and still in business), the most extensive and interesting.

14. Glover, Dorothy, and Graham Greene. Victorian Detective Fiction: A Catalogue of the Collection Made by Dorothy Glover and Graham Greene. Bibliographically arranged by Eric Osborne and introduced by John Carter. London: The Bodley Head, 1966. xviii, 149p. Index.

According to Graham Greene's preface, an allusion by Sergeant Cuff in The Moonstone (a novel claimed by many historians to be the first English detective novel) to earlier fiction about detectives led Greene and Glover to begin collecting among the Victorians. The result is a catalogue of 471 numbered entries, arranged alphabetically by author and fully described bibliographically. The annotations, principally identifying the detective involved, are by Glover. According to Carter's introduction (a charming account of the early days of detective-fiction collecting), the terminal date is 1900, though a few 1901 publications are to be found.
Some of the books identified as detective fiction may be controversial choices. Dickens's Nicholas Nickleby is included, along with the expected Bleak House and Edwin

Drood. Some of the more prolific authors who make appearances are Fortuné Du Biosgobey, Dick Donovan, M. E. Braddon, Fergus Hume, Lawrence Lynch, and "Waters," as well as Anna Katharine Green, Wilkie Collins, and A. Conan Doyle.

Featured as an appendix is "The Publishing History of Fergus Hume's The Mystery of a Hansom Cab," by Eric Sinclair Bell. There are indexes of detectives, illustrators, and titles. The detective index includes the following categories in addition to personal names: Bow Street Runners, female detectives, journalists, lawyers, and physicians and surgeons.

15. Gribbin, Lenore S. Who's Whodunit (University of North Carolina Library Studies, No. 5). Chapel Hill: University of North Carolina, 1969. ix, 174p.

Aiming to "present the names of all American and British authors of book-length detective stories from 1845 to 1961" (page v), this scholarly work may still be of value to librarians as a name authority list, but as a directory of mystery writers' pseudonyms it has been pretty well superseded by the Hubin bibliography (see #18). Printed sources for the pseudonyms are indicated. Some misinformation from these sources is recommunicated, including the notoriously persistent misidentification of Jack Vance as a pseudonym of Henry Kuttner.

16. Hagen, Ordean A. Who Done It?: A Guide to Detective, Mystery and Suspense Fiction. New York: Bowker, 1969. xx, 834p. Index.

This pioneering work of crime-fiction bibliography was of inestimable value to readers and collectors in the field despite an incredibly large number of errors of fact and omission. Its main section, an attempt to list alphabetically by author every book of mystery and detective fiction ever published in English, fell far short of its goal but became the basis for the Hubin bibliography (see #18), which now completely supersedes it. Other features include a subject guide to mysteries (limited but still useful), a chapter on screen adaptations, a listing of mystery plays, a listing of mysteries set in various countries, a directory of continuing characters in mystery fiction, a bibliography of anthologies and collections, a list of award-winning mysteries, a bibliography of secondary sources, and a section of miscellaneous information. All these features include some useful information, though many of the topics are covered better elsewhere. The final section is a title index to the main bibliography, also superseded by Hubin.

Hagen, who died shortly before the publication of his monumental effort, was the "point man" of mystery bibliography. Though others have rendered much of his work outmoded, he has an honored place in the history of mystery scholarship.

17. Herman, Linda, and Beth Stiel. Corpus Delicti of Mystery Fiction: A Guide to the Body of the Crime. Metuchen, New Jersey: Scarecrow, 1974. viii, 180p.

This reference guide to mystery fiction is very much for the beginner in the field, with little to offer the initiate. The reliance on secondary sources is heavy, and misprints (for example, Ruth Fenison, James Sandow, Jon J. Breen) abound. After a few introductory chapters of definition, history, and bibliography, the main body of the work is a guide to fifty representative authors, largely a good selection. The work's brevity, however, limits its usefulness.

There are some inconsistencies and eccentricities in the way writers are categorized. Robert van Gulik and the Lockridges seem dubiously cast as police procedural writers, and their inclusion flatly contradicts a definition (also questionable) elsewhere in the volume that states procedurals have no one individual dominating the detection. This definition would also seem to eliminate J. J. Marric's (John Creasey's) Gideon, Dell Shannon's Luis Mendoza, and Georges Simenon's Maigret.

Although the author checklists are of some use, the short introductions to the checklists are often ill written and uninformative. The whole project has the aura of a rush job.

18. Hubin, Allen J. The Bibliography of Crime Fiction, 1749-1975. Del Mar: University Extension, University of California, San Diego, in cooperation with Publisher's Inc., 1979. xiv, 697p. Index.

Using the bibliography in Ordean Hagen's Who Done It? (see #16) as a starting point, Hubin has updated, corrected, and improved that work into one of the truly indispensable volumes of crime-fiction scholarship. Entries are listed alphabetically by author. In a departure from Hagen, works written by an author under different names are listed separately under the individual bylines, with cross-references to the true author's name and to other pseudonyms. In another improvement, Hubin identifies series characters appearing in more than one book. Unexamined titles whose appropriateness to the list is in doubt are preceded by a dash. Both American and British first editions are noted by publisher and year. A full title index follows the main list.

Inevitably, a few errors and omissions have crept into this massive project. For example, Alan Green's What a Body is in the title index but does not turn up in the main list under Green's name. But compared with the galloping errata of Who Done It? and Barzun and Taylor's A Catalogue of Crime (see #10), the mistakes are few indeed. Hubin, drawing on what is probably the greatest of all mystery-fiction collections, has come about as close as humanly possible to achieving the goal of listing every volume of mystery and detective fiction published in English. The volume also includes more pseudonym information related to the mystery field than has ever appeared in one source.

19. Lofts, W. O. G., and D. J. Adley. The Men Behind Boys' Fiction. Introduction by Leslie Charteris. London: Howard Baker, 1970. 361p.

Many of the writers listed in this biographical diction-ary of boys'-story bylines (all from British periodicals, mostly published by Amalgamated Press and Fleetway Publi-cations) did not write detective fiction. But the volume is worth including here mainly for its identification of the various writers who did Sexton Blake stories over the years. Some of the names listed are merely identified by the papers they contributed to; others are identified as house names or pen names; and some are given a paragraph or two of biography. Among the Sexton Blake chroniclers cited are Barry Perowne (Philip Atkey), John Creasey, Michael Moorcock (whose one Blake novel appeared under the house name Desmond Reid), and Jack Trevor Story. Other adult writers who contributed to juvenile papers are included, among them Leslie Charteris, Peter Cheyney, and even Agatha Christie.

20. McCormick, Donald. Who's Who in Spy Fiction. Lon-

don: Elm Tree, 1977. 216p. Bibl. American edition,
New York: Taplinger, 1977. 216p. Bibl.

McCormick's biographical dictionary of espionage
writers is a highly readable, very personal reference book,
all the more entertaining for being so opinionated. Following a fifteen-page introduction, McCormick offers about ninety
entries, most covering a page or two with some major writers
getting more extended coverage (for example, four pages
each for Ian Fleming, John Le Carré, and Eric Ambler).
Many writers are not likely to turn up in other biographical
sources, including Ken Follett (and this was published before
The Eye of the Needle), Angus Ross, Brian Garfield (who
did not make Encyclopedia of Mystery and Detection, #31),
and Philip McCutchan. The entries feature both biographical
information and critical comments, and many include quotations from the authors discussed. In an appendix, McCormick
offers a glossary of espionage terminology.
Unfortunately, this is one of those many mystery
reference sources that are full of mistakes, typified by references to Edgar Allen Poe and Arthur Sarsfield Wade (as
Sax Rohmer's real name). There are also some rather glaring omissions, notably Donald Hamilton and Manning Coles.
McCormick's entry on E. Howard Hunt seems unduly harsh.
Whatever his personal activities as a CIA agent and Watergate figure, Hunt is a much better writer than McCormick's
comments suggest.

21. Mundell, E. H. , Jr. , and G. Jay Rausch. The Detective
Short Story: A Bibliography and Index (Bibliographic Series,
No. 14). Manhattan: Kansas State University Library, 1974.
iv, 493p.

The main section arranges single-author collections
alphabetically by the author's name, listing American and
English first editions, series characters involved, and detective stories included in the volume. In cases where not all
of the tales qualify as detection (for example, in some of
the collections by Leslie Charteris and Cornell Woolrich),
only bona fide detective stories are listed. Stories reprinted
from other collections are not listed. Other sections cover
Sherlockiana and Poeiana, detective-story anthologies, single-
author collections and anthologies of "secret service" stories,
collections of problems and puzzles (for example, The Baffle
Book), semi-nonfictional collections of "detective experiences"
(mostly nineteenth-century), and titles not examined. An

index of detectives and agents (not confined to series characters) identifies their authors. Finally, there is an author index of individual stories, referring to the numbered entries of the collections in which they appear.

Aside from covering more recent material, the Mundell and Rausch work differs from Ellery Queen's 1942 bibliography, The Detective Short Story (see #26) in two ways: it includes individual story titles, which Queen did not do, and it is not a fully descriptive bibliography, as Queen's is.

This is a unique and invaluable source for locating stories in collections. One error noted was the misidentification of van Gulik's Judge Dee books as collections. Though they usually involve three different cases, the cases are intermingled in the course of the narrative, and the books (with the exception of Judge Dee at Work and The Monkey and the Tiger) are clearly novels rather than collections.

22. Nieminski, John. EQMM 350: An Author/Title Index to Ellery Queen's Mystery Magazine, Fall 1941 Through January 1973. White Bear Lake, Minnesota: The Armchair Detective, 1974. 116p.

The main list, by author, includes 4,212 numbered entries for stories from the first 350 issues of EQMM. Series characters are noted at the beginning of the author entry. Cross-references are provided for pseudonyms. Reprints are noted, and original titles are given for stories that editor Queen (Frederic Dannay) renamed, not an infrequent occurrence. Features, articles, quizzes, columns, and verse are included in the index as well as stories. Nieminski also provides a title index and separate lists of title changes, series characters, and translators. In the appendixes, there are finding tools for various types of features (true crime, poems and verse, quizzes and puzzles, etc.) in the main list, plus an index to cartoonists (not in the main list), giving the issues to which they contributed. The final appendixes locate Sherlockiana and parodies and pastiches, organized by target.

The only criticism of Nieminski's remarkably thorough and useful index is that it is seven years out of date (at this writing).

23. Nieminski, John. The Saint Magazine Index: Authors and Titles, Spring 1953-October 1967 (The Unicorn Indexes

to the Mystery/Detective Magazines). Evansville, Indiana:
Cook & McDowell, 1980. 68p.

The only thing that keeps this index from being as
impressive as EQMM 350 (see #22) is that The Saint Magazine enjoyed a much shorter run. The format is almost
identical, with 1,334 numbered entries arranged by author,
followed by a title index. As with EQMM 350, reprint title
changes, series characters, and pseudonyms are noted. The
appendixes identify title changes, series characters, articles,
essays, and features; true crime, book reviews, quizzes and
puzzles; and Sherlockiana.

24. Parish, James Robert, and Michael R. Pitts. The
Great Spy Pictures. Metuchen, New Jersey: Scarecrow,
1974. viii, 585p. Illus., bibl.

Here is a treasure trove of information about the
spy on film. Following a 347-page history of the genre,
463 entries are presented alphabetically by title, giving running time, date, virtually complete credits, and a brief plot
summary and critical analysis. The staggering amount of
data in the annotations is truly impressive. Quotes from
reviews augment the authors' own comments. Numerous
stills from the films are included.
Appendixes include lists of radio and TV spy-adventure
shows (unannotated), a selected 38-page bibliography of spy
novels by T. Allan Taylor (the introduction to which also
cites many nonfiction works on the espionage field), and nine
pages of checklists of spy-novel series.
The only objection is to the title, an utter misnomer.
As the annotations themselves clearly indicate, most of the
films described here are far from great. Among the gems
discussed are Charlie Chan in Secret Service, Air Raid
Wardens, Arizona Bushwhackers, G-Men Versus the Black
Dragon (among other Republic serials), The Spy with a Cold
Nose, and Tarzan's Desert Mystery. With inclusions like
these, the book sometimes reads like a Harvey Medved production.

25. Pitts, Michael R. Famous Movie Detectives. Metuchen,
New Jersey: Scarecrow, 1979. ix, 357p. Illus., bibl., index.

Like the author's collaboration with James Robert

Parish on spy films (see #24), this is a vast storehouse of information. In separate chapters, Pitts traces the screen careers of seventeen detectives, among them Charlie Chan, Ellery Queen, Hildegarde Withers, Michael Shayne, Philo Vance, The Saint, Sam Spade, and The Thin Man. An eighteenth chapter treats seven others more briefly. After a narrative history of the sleuth's career, the films are listed chronologically with date, running time, and complete credits. A bibliography of the book appearances of the detectives is included, followed by an index of names and titles. The books on film detectives by William K. Everson (see #40) and Jon Tuska (see #59) include more interesting critical commentary and generally more impressive writing, but the filmographies and extensive data make this volume a better bet for reference use.

Most of the errors noted have to do with films' literary sources. Frederic Dannay was originally named Daniel Nathan, not vice versa as indicated here. The date of the first Mike Shayne novel is given as 1934, rather than 1939. There is a fascinating reference to Harry Stephen Reefer (!) on page 207. And the bibliography lists as being about Ellery Queen a number of paperback originals signed by EQ (author) in which EQ (detective) does not appear.

26. Queen, Ellery (Frederic Dannay and Manfred B. Lee). The Detective Short Story: A Bibliography. Boston: Little, Brown, 1942. 146p. Index.

In the 1930s, Frederic Dannay (the editor-scholar half of the Ellery Queen collaboration) began to put together the world's greatest collection of first editions of books of detective short stories. Two of the products of that ambitious project were the seminal anthology 101 Years' Entertainment, published in 1941 to commemorate the hundredth anniversary of Poe's first detective story, and this meticulous descriptive bibliography.

The entries are arranged alphabetically by author. Generally, only the first edition is listed, though first American or first British are noted in cases where there is a title change or a change in contents. Series characters are noted. Some entries are annotated, generally with notes bearing on their eligibility for the list, identification of detective stories included in mixed collections, or identification of volumes of particular historical importance. Few of the annotations are critical. An important feature is the recognition of Chinese detective fiction, rarely touched on in discussions of the genre up to this time.

Following the main listing, anthologies are listed in chronological order. An index of detectives and criminals includes names, nicknames (for example, The Rule of Thumb Detective), and categories (Women Detectives, Secret Service Agents, Boy Detectives). There is a separate index of anthology editors. The compiler generally takes a purist approach to the items to be included, though crook stories are admitted as the mirror image of detective stories.

Obviously, this is one of the basic items for the mystery reference shelf.

27. Queen, Ellery (Frederic Dannay and Manfred B. Lee). Queen's Quorum: A History of the Detective-Crime Short Story as Revealed by the 106 Most Important Books Published in This Field Since 1845. Boston: Little, Brown, 1951. ix, 132p. Illus. , index. Revised edition, New York: Biblo and Tannen, 1969. 146p. Illus. , index.

Unlike the Queen bibliography (see #26), this historical-critical listing is not confined to detective and crook stories but takes in the whole range of the crime-mystery-suspense field. The numbered entries are arranged chronologically with a linking narration explaining each volume's importance. The three criteria for inclusion are historical importance, literary quality, and value as a collector's item, and symbols are used to identify which of the criteria each item fulfills. There is a single index to authors, titles, and detectives. The first edition of this significant work carries the list through number 106, Lawrence G. Blochman's Diagnosis: Homicide (1950).

Earlier versions of Queen's Quorum appeared in Ellery Queen's Mystery Magazine (June 1949 through July 1950) and in Queen's anthology Twentieth Century Detective Stories (1948). Supplements appeared in EQMM for November and December 1968, and these were incorporated in the 1969 revised edition. Last volume included to date is number 125, Harry Kemelman's The Nine Mile Walk (1967).

28. Radcliffe, Elsa J. Gothic Novels of the Twentieth Century: An Annotated Bibliography. Metuchen, New Jersey: Scarecrow, 1979. xix, 272p. Index.

Similar in format to Myron J. Smith's Cloak-and-Dagger Bibliography (see #30), Radcliffe's work is also unique and equally eccentric and error-prone. The 1973 numbered entries are alphabetical by author with an index by title. Some are annotated and graded on quality A through F. Many of the paperback gothics of the sixties and seventies are discussed here and nowhere else.

Errors are rampant. Radcliffe fails to identify some rather well-known pseudonyms (for example, Kieran Abbey = Helen Reilly, Jennie Melville = Gwendoline Butler); doesn't supply a death date for Charlotte Armstrong; misnames Michael Avallone's private eye as Ed Noone (and lists some of his cases for no apparent reason); implies that John Dickson Carr sometimes wrote as John D. Carr; includes a baffling blind cross-reference from Cecil, Henry, pseud., to Keller, David H.; totally omits Mignon G. Eberhart; and includes some obviously inappropriate authors (Gardner F. Fox, Carter Brown, A. B. Cox, Josephine Bell).

Radcliffe's opinions may confound readers even more than her factual howlers. For some reason, she is extremely cool toward Phyllis A. Whitney and Daphne du Maurier (an entry that made at least this reader's blood boil). She seems to prefer Elsie Lee to either. The choice of what will be annotated seems arbitrary in the extreme. Some acknowledged classics are listed only, while potboilers are discussed and graded. Many of the annotations are neither informative nor well wrought. This is a book that is valuable only because there is nothing else like it.

29. Reilly, John M., ed. Twentieth-Century Crime and Mystery Writers (Twentieth Century Writers of the English Language). London: Macmillan, 1980. xxiv, 1,568p. Bibl. American edition, New York: St. Martin's, 1980. xxiv, 1,568p. Bibl.

More than 600 writers of crime fiction are covered in this massive tome, the latest addition to the permanent mystery reference shelf. The entries follow the format of the publisher's Contemporary Writers series, including the following information on each author covered: a who's-who-style biography, a list of works (divided here between crime and noncrime writings and usually by pseudonyms used), citations of published bibliography and location of manuscript collection (if any), a short statement by the subject in some cases, and finally a signed critical summary, ranging from a paragraph to about a page and a half for major figures (Patricia Highsmith's entry runs nearly two pages). Following the main section of English-language writers of this century, appendixes cover nine nineteenth-century pioneers and sixteen foreign-language writers. (Two of these, though, Robert van Gulik and Janwillem van de Wetering, actually write in English.)

There are both famous names and unknowns among the
critical contributors, but all are well qualified and most do
a creditable job of capturing the essence of their subjects.
There is an occasional aura of puffery in the air, however.
Of the half-dozen novelists treated who are also on the project's advisory board, only Dennis Lynds (subject, as "Michael Collins," of a balanced and perceptive essay by Richard
A. Carpenter) gets other than a totally glowing report card.
And having Ray Russell write a piece on William F. Nolan
that is exceeded in fulsomeness of praise only by Nolan's
essay on Russell tends to elevate the eyebrow.

The authors who choose to comment on their own
works often provide some real insights. See, for example,
the entries on Martha Albrand, Glyn Carr, and Peter Dick-
inson. They sometimes contradict the critics. While Sara
Woods says in her self-portrait that "what I am most interested in is the development of character" (page 1507), Joanne
Harack Hayne says in the critical squib, "Characterization
is not Woods' strong point...." (page 1508).

The most prolific contributor is H. R. F. Keating,
who also stands out for the quality of his critical comments.
Melvyn Barnes covers a wide range of writers in fine fashion
and is generally livelier here than in his Best Detective Fiction (see #9). Charles Shibuk, Mary Helen Becker, E. F.
Bleiler (specializing in old-timers), and Mary Ann Grochowski
are other mainstays. Art Scott contributes some fine work,
specializing in paperback-original writers. Well-known mystery writers who contribute include Dorothy B. Hughes,
Robert B. Parker, Bill Pronzini, and Edward D. Hoch.
Francis M. Nevins, Jr., offers good discussions of some of
his usual subjects: Michael Avallone, Harry Stephen Keeler,
Erle Stanley Gardner, Ellery Queen, Cornell Woolrich. The
critic who most consistently disappoints is Herbert Harris,
whose brief notes (mostly on relatively obscure British
writers) sometimes avoid evaluation altogether.

The bibliographies are valuable but sometimes incomplete, especially in their listings of uncollected short stories.
The inclusion of non-crime-fiction writings by the subjects,
though in the case of a prolific writer like Isaac Asimov it
can become faintly comical, gives the bibliographic section
an added dimension, one not present in the Hubin bibliography
(see #18).

The subjects are generally well chosen, with only a
few really glaring omissions--David Alexander, Howard
Browne, and Victoria Holt are three. The inclusion of
writers like William Brittain, Jack Ritchie, and Joyce Har-
rington, known exclusively for short stories at the time of
compilation, is a valuable plus. One surprising listing is

Hugh Marlowe--he unquestionably belongs, but why under that name rather than the better-known Jack Higgins or Harry Patterson? Of course, there are cross-references.

The work is marred by one incredibly glaring error. The entry on Jack Webb assumes that the novelist and the TV actor-producer are the same man. They are not, and that fact has been well known in the mystery field for years. This howler, though, is an exception in a basically reliable source whose errors of commission are rare. In fact, one persistent error is implicitly corrected here--the identification of British novelist Miles Tripp with American novelist Michael Brett. Though Tripp coincidentally has written some novels under the name Michael Brett, the author of the Pete McGrath books is a different man. The assertion that they are the same has persisted as recently as the Hubin bibliography.

30. Smith, Myron J., Jr. Cloak-and-Dagger Bibliography: An Annotated Guide to Spy Fiction, 1937-1975. Metuchen, New Jersey: Scarecrow, 1976. xi, 225p. Index.

As the only work of its kind, this volume has undeniable usefulness, and it has the idiosyncratic charm of many single-author reference works. A not-very-informative introduction precedes a listing of 1,675 numbered entries, arranged alphabetically by author. An index by title follows. Most of the entries are annotated, usually descriptively rather than critically. Some annoyingly facetious terminology (for example, references to "nasties" and "Chinamen") creeps into the annotations. Symbols identify titles with humor, low sex quotient, and suitability for young adults. Most of the expected authors are covered, though Dennis Wheatley seems a surprising omission.

The work has many errors. Michael Avallone's Missing is misidentified as an Ed Noon novel. Per Wahlöö is credited as sole author of the Martin Beck novels, which he wrote in collaboration with his wife, Maj Sjöwall. Erskine Childers's Riddle of the Sands (1903) is dated 1940 with no reference to an earlier publication. Patricia McGerr is called McGeer, and Michael Avallone becomes Avallon. Finally, since Stephen Marlowe's Chester Drum began his career in 1955, well before the onset of Bond mania, it seems doubtful he was intended as a parody of 007.

31. Steinbrunner, Chris, and Otto Penzler. Encyclopedia of

Mystery and Detection. Marvin Lachman and Charles Shibuk, Senior Editors. New York: McGraw-Hill, 1976. 435p. Illus. , bibl.

This ambitious compilation ranks with the Hubin bibliography (see #18) and Reilly's Twentieth-Century Crime and Mystery Writers (see #29) as one of indispensable reference sources in the field. It was the first comprehensive reference on the mystery genre that was generally reliable for its accuracy--no small achievement.

The entries are in one alphabet with no index but ample cross-references. Most of the articles are under the names of authors and major characters. They offer brief identifications and biographical details, sometimes a critical comment, and checklists in the case of major figures. Though the articles on individuals are unsigned, there are several signed survey articles: "Locked-Room Mysteries" (Hans Stefan Santesson), "Collecting Detective Fiction" (Norman S. Nolan), "Orientals, Sinister" (Robert E. Briney), "Pulp Magazines" (Ron Goulart), "Radio Detectives" (Daniel J. Morrow), and "Scientific Detectives" (Sam Moskowitz).

Many of the entries include information on film adaptations as well as book appearances. Illustrations are many and varied, including magazine illustrations, book covers and jackets, portraits of authors, and stage and movie stills.

As might be expected in a multiauthor encyclopedia, there is some unevenness in the writing. While some articles remain strictly factual when a measure of critical analysis would be welcome, others do a good job of combining the biographical and the critical, notably an excellent article on Erle Stanley Gardner.

With few errors to grumble about, we can still point out some rather notable omissions from the compendium: Brian Garfield, Alistair MacLean, Patricia McGerr, Ellis Peters, Kelley Roos, Richard S. Prather, and the oddly forgotten Clifford Knight, who was also ignored by Barzun and Taylor in A Catalogue of Crime (see #10).

This volume won the Mystery Writers of America Edgar award for the best biographical-critical book of 1976.

32.   Steinbrunner, Chris; Charles Shibuk; Otto Penzler; Marvin Lachman; and Francis M. Nevins, Jr.   Detectionary. Lock Haven, Pennsylvania: Hammermill Paper Company, 1971.   xiv, 590p.   Commercial edition: Otto Penzler, Chris Steinbrunner, and Marvin Lachman, eds.   Conceived and produced by Mill Roseman.   Woodstock, New York: Overlook, 1977.   xi, 290p.   Illus. , bibl. , index.

Here is a volume with a curious publishing history and credits as complicated as a Hollywood movie. The first edition was a privately printed paperback of which most of the copies were lost. The hardcover edition is virtually identical in content, though the author checklists in the index have been expanded and updated and the layout has been adjusted to a larger page.

The book is divided into four sections: detectives, rogues and helpers, cases, and movies. In the first two sections, the fictional characters are identified with their creators and described in a brief thumbnail sketch. The section of cases gives brief synopses of some major novels and stories involving the characters in the first two sections. These are arranged alphabetically by title. The movie section is arranged by character or series and briefly discusses the screen adaptations of the various detectives or villains. Generally, the annotations are descriptive rather than critical. Symbols within the sections serve as cross-references from one section to another. The index is arranged by author, listing characters discussed and representative titles. The book is illustrated with a movie still on every page, but the stills are identified only by title, studio, and year, leading to some maddening sessions of trying to remember the name of a particular actor. Also, the still never coincides with the matter being discussed on the page.

Many of the same authors involved in the Detectionary later compiled Encyclopedia of Mystery and Detection (see #31), a much superior work that to some degree supersedes this one. Still, the Detectionary is entertaining, and it has the special attribute of identifying some obscure characters not likely to turn up elsewhere, such as Carolyn Wells's Bert Bayliss, Erle Stanley Gardner's Sidney Zoom, Jack Ehrlich's Robert W. Flick, Robert O. Saber's Carl Good, Harry Stephen Keeler's Angus MacWhorter, and D. I. Champion's Rex Sackler. Unfortunately, though, there are no clues given for tracking down the magazine appearances of some of the little-known sleuths.

33. Stevenson, W. B. Detective Fiction (Reader's Guides, Third Series). Cambridge: University Press for the National Book League, 1958. 32p. Index.

Aiming for "a basic list of writers of detective fiction," Stevenson offers a short introduction followed by a briefly annotated reading list in three parts: The Old Masters, The Moderns, and Books About Detective Fiction. The listing is by author, with an index by title. The selections are influenced to a degree by availability at the time of the pamphlet's publication.

Stevenson's selection seems sound enough, though the annotations are unscintillating and sometimes misleading. For example, Van Dine's The Bishop Murder Case is said to be "free from the authors [sic] later mannerisms" (page 14). Van Dine never wrote an unmannered book in his life. And few of the Uncle Abner stories from Melville Davisson Post's original volume were reprinted in EQMM, though Stevenson's annotation suggests otherwise. In an odd categorization, Dashiell Hammett appears with the Old Masters, Agatha Christie and John Rhode with the Moderns.

34. Stilwell, Steven A. The Armchair Detective Index (Volumes 1-10) 1967-1977. Introduction by Allen J. Hubin. New York: The Armchair Detective, 1979. 64p.

Since its debut in 1967, some of the best writing about the mystery and detective-fiction field has appeared in the genre's pioneering fanzine, The Armchair Detective, edited by Allen J. Hubin. Stilwell's very welcome compilation indexes the first ten years of TAD by author, title, and subject. Even the letter column has been analyzed by writer and subject, giving even greater access to comment. TAD's more prolific contributors have included Jacques Barzun and Wendell Hertig Taylor, Robert E. Briney, J. R. Christopher, J. Randolph Cox, Fred Dueren, William K. Everson, R. W. Hays, Amnon Kabatchnik, Veronica M. S. Kennedy, Marvin Lachman, Edward S. Lauterbach, Dick Lochte, Frank D. McSherry, Jr., Francis M. Nevins, Jr., William F. Nolan, and (above all) Charles Shibuk, a contributor to every issue from the first to the latest.

35. Symons, Julian. The Hundred Best Crime Stories. London: The Sunday Times, 1959. 21p. Illus.

In compiling this excellent and well-annotated list, Symons consulted a number of eminent critics and novelists, including Anthony Boucher, James Sandoe, Howard Haycraft, Raymond Chandler, Ellery Queen, Rex Stout, Agatha Christie, Henry Cecil, Nicholas Blake, C. P. Snow, and Cyril Hare. The compiler, though, takes responsibility for the final selection. The entries are in four categories: Begetters, The Age of the Great Detectives, Novels of Action, and The

Modern Crime Novel. Items within the categories are presented chronologically. Portraits of some of the authors are included.

Most of the selections are the expected ones. Among the more surprising inclusions are Edgar Wallace's The Crimson Circle (1922), Erle Stanley Gardner's The Case of the Sleepwalker's Niece (1936), William Faulkner's Sanctuary (1931), John Mair's Never Come Back (1941), Victor Canning's Venetian Blind (1951), Hugh Walpole's Above the Dark Circus (1931), and Ernest Raymond's We the Accused (1935). Sapper's Bull-dog Drummond (1920) is included for historical reasons, though Symons hasn't a single good word to say for it.   †

III † SPECIAL SUBJECTS

36. Butler, William Vivyan.   The Durable Desperadoes.
Preface by Anthony Lejeune.   London: Macmillan, 1973.
288p. Bibl. , index.

This is the only book-length study of crime fiction's
criminal heroes and edge-of-the-law adventurers.   Among
the Gentleman Outlaws Butler discusses are E. W. Hornung's
Raffles, Sapper's Bulldog Drummond, Leslie Charteris's
The Saint, John Creasey's The Toff and The Baron, Bruce
Graeme's Blackshirt, and Berkeley Gray's Norman Conquest.
The emphasis is decidedly British, with the American equiv-
alents--Frank L. Packard's Jimmie Dale, Maxwell Grant's
The Shadow, Jack Boyle's Boston Blackie--either mentioned
only in passing or not discussed at all.   Unsurprisingly, the
first ancestor Butler identifies is Robin Hood.
Butler does a beautiful job of capturing the essence
of his subjects in such paragraphs as this:

Flippant repartee was not the only sine qua non
of the Gentleman Outlaw. Standard equipment included a faultless evening suit; a bizarre soubriquet,
breathed in whispers throughout the awestruck
Underworld (Conquest's, incidentally, was 1066);
an automatic pistol and, in the case of the amateur
cracksmen, a black mask of the finest crêpe,
always worn when flitting around baronesses' bed-
rooms removing pearls, but usually discarded for
such jobs as laughingly tipping arch-fiends into the
Thames [page 23].

This is altogether a splendid book, as entertaining as

the tales it discusses and unique in the ground it covers. Butler offers some of the best writing extant about Raffles, The Saint, and Bulldog Drummond, and very nearly the only writing about Blackshirt, The Toff, and The Baron.

37. Carter, John. Collecting Detective Fiction (Aspects of Book-Collecting). London: Constable, n. d. (1938). 31p. (numbered 33-63). Notes.

Carter's pioneering discussion of collecting detective fiction, a historical survey with bibliographic citations in footnotes, is here reprinted in pamphlet form from its original appearance in the collection New Paths in Book Collecting (Constable, 1934), edited by Carter. It was also reprinted in Haycraft's The Art of the Mystery Story (see #89).

38. Cawelti, John G. Adventure, Mystery, and Romance: Formula Stories as Art and Popular Culture. Chicago: University of Chicago Press, 1976. viii, 336p. Notes, index.

In his discussion of formulas in popular fiction, Cawelti covers the western and the best-selling "social melodrama" (exemplified by Irving Wallace), but his main focus is on crime fiction: the Godfather-type gangster novel, the classical detective story, and the hardboiled private-eye story. Among the authors he discusses at some length are Poe, Christie (closely analyzing the successful use of her formula in An Overdose of Death and its failure in Third Girl), Sayers (concentrating on The Nine Tailors), Simenon, Hammett, Chandler, and Spillane. In the section on the latter, Cawelti reveals the limits of his knowledge of the genre by the misstatement that Brett Halliday and Richard Prather are "prolific hacks who more or less imitate the Spillane recipe" (page 183).
Cawelti makes some genuinely good points about formula. Unfortunately, his rather verbose writing style makes the book tough sledding at times.

39. Champigny, Robert. What Will Have Happened: A Philosophical and Technical Essay on Mystery Stories. Bloomington: Indiana University Press, 1977. viii, 183p. Bibl. , index.

I am unqualified to judge the interest of this book to

philosophers, but it is safe to say that few general detective-
fiction buffs will get much out of it. As an example of
the almost impenetrable style, the first two sentences of the
prologue will serve: "Narrative sentences may be interpreted
as indicating historical or fictional events. In the former
case, what is narrated is spatiotemporally related to the
interpreter's own incarnation; in the latter case, it is not"
(page 3).

Though it doesn't help much, Champigny refers to
many authors and titles in the course of his argument. Among
those most frequently alluded to are Carr, Chandler, Chesterton, Christie, Leblanc, Poe, Queen, and Joel Townsley
Rogers, whose The Red Right Hand is discussed in considerable detail.

40. Everson, William K. The Detective in Film. Secau-
cus, New Jersey: Citadel, 1972. v, 247p. Illus., index.

Claiming only a casual knowledge of their literary
antecedents, Everson traces the history of screen sleuths
from the earliest Sherlock Holmes film in 1903 to such early-
seventies features as Klute and Cotton Comes to Harlem.
Though other writers have gone over this ground since,
Everson's account remains the best, for his smooth and
civilized writing style as much as his encyclopedic knowledge
of movie history and his sound critical perspective. The
volume is generously illustrated with stills.

Following an excellent chapter summarizing Holmes's
screen career, Everson covers the silent period (not the
most fertile ground for detection for obvious reasons); a
trio of classic mystery films (The Kennel Murder Case,
Green for Danger, and The Maltese Falcon); the early talkies
(a natural for immobile Q-and-A); Bulldog Drummond (the
only sleuth save Holmes to rate a chapter of his own); the
Oriental detectives (Charlie Chan, Mr. Moto, Mr. Wong);
gentleman private eyes (Philo Vance, Nick Charles, The
Saint, The Falcon, Perry Mason--really a lawyer--and
others); gangster and FBI films; the British output (an entertaining chapter covering many obscure films not discussed
elsewhere); detectives in Hitchcock's films (surprisingly un-
important); comedy and camp (discussing the detectival exploits of Laurel and Hardy, Buster Keaton, Bob Hope, and
other screen comedians, as well as superhero detectives);
and hardboiled private eyes (surprisingly including Ellery
Queen, surely a gentleman sleuth, in addition to Philip Marlowe, Mike Hammer, Tony Rome, and the expected choices).

One reason for the value of Everson's work is that he does not confine himself to well-known series sleuths but covers film detection generally.

41.   Geherin, David.   Sons of Sam Spade: The Private Eye Novel in the 70s.   New York: Ungar, 1980.   vii, 168p. Notes, bibl., index.

The private-eye novel has enjoyed something of a renaissance in the past ten years.   Geherin discusses three writers who have taken varying approaches to the established form: Robert B. Parker (continuation), Roger L. Simon (updating), and Andrew Bergman (parody).   About half the space is spent on Parker, five of whose books are covered (through The Judas Goat) to three by Simon and two by Bergman.

Geherin draws a strong parallel between Parker and Hemingway, which may explain some of what is good and much that is exasperating in the writing of Spenser's creator. Valid as it all may be, the close examination of Parker's novels gets somewhat tiresome and seems to feed the author's pretentiousness.   The section on Simon, a far less self-important writer and a more original one, is more entertaining.   The section on Bergman is also good, though it points up the dubious value of undiluted plot summary.   Solutions are freely given, but in the context of these three writers it doesn't seem to matter much.

On balance, this is a readable and worthwhile book, full of good points.

42.   Gilbert, Elliot L.   The World of Mystery Fiction: A Guide.   Preface by Ellery Queen.   Del Mar: University Extension, University of California, San Diego, in cooperation with Publisher's Inc., 1978.   vi, 153p.   Bibl.

Published to accompany the author's anthology The World of Mystery Fiction as the basis for a formal university course in the genre, this is very much a textbook, complete with objectives, assignments, and review questions at the end of each chapter.   These features may be off-putting to the general reader, to whom Gilbert's work has much to offer.   He is the rare academic commentator on mystery fiction who knows the field in depth and is able to discuss it without crossing the line into scholarly hair-splitting.

In an unusual progression, Gilbert starts with the

hardboiled school of Hammett, contrasting it with the world
of classical detection, then proceeds to examine the historical roots of detective fiction, paralleling Vidocq and the
Continental Op as being equally remote from the figure of
the Great Detective. Gilbert then devotes chapters to Poe,
Charles Dickens's The Mystery of Edwin Drood, Conan Doyle
and Holmes, the tradition of the gothic novel as continued
and adapted by Mary Roberts Rinehart in The Circular Staircase, the locked room, the "Golden Age" of detection (concentrating on Simenon, Sayers, and Queen), Hammett's The
Maltese Falcon, spy fiction, "The Limits of Detection" (concentrating on Jorge Luis Borges's "Death and the Compass"),
and recent appearances of the detective figure in dramatic
works generally outside the realm of detective fiction as
such.

43. Goulart, Ron. Cheap Thrills: An Informal History of
the Pulp Magazines. New Rochelle, New York: Arlington
House, 1972. 192p. Illus.

Goulart's highly readable but frustratingly sketchy and
undocumented account of the pulps does not deal exclusively
with mysteries, though they are prominent in chapters on
The Shadow, various masked heroes, Doc Savage, "Special
Agents," and "Dime Detectives." The latter chapter deals
with the development of Black Mask and such writers as
Carroll John Daly (quoted to good effect), Hammett, Chandler,
and Norbert Davis. Goulart closes the chapter with an
account of Robert Leslie Bellem's irresistible Hollywood
detective Dan Turner. (Typical quote: "If there's anything
I dislike, it's having some misguided skirt probing my sacro-
iliac with a rodney" [page 133]).
The final chapter (all too short!) includes reminiscences of such pulp veterans as Norman Daniels, Frederick
Nebel, Richard Wormser, Bruno Fischer, Richard Deming,
and Howard Browne. The illustrations include black-and-
white reproductions of pulp covers.

44. Grossvogel, David L. Mystery and Its Fictions: From
Oedipus to Agatha Christie. Baltimore: Johns Hopkins
University Press, 1979. xi, 203p. Bibl. , index.

This academic study of the element of mystery in
literature seems to be slanted toward readers and scholars
of the detective story via its subtitle (evoking the magic name

of Christie) and promotion. But most of the chapters--about such writers as Sophocles, Dostoevsky, Camus, Pirandello, and Kafka--are not about mystery fiction per se. The chapter on Christie, discussing The Mysterious Affair at Styles in some detail, is remarkably unfriendly to the writer whose name is being used to sell the book. There is also a chapter on Poe's "The Purloined Letter."

My reaction to this book can be summed up in three words: "Life's too short."

45. Gruber, Frank. The Pulp Jungle. Los Angeles: Sherbourne, 1967. 189p.

Gruber's reminiscences of the pulp days are expanded here from the introduction to Brass Knuckles (1966), a collection of his Oliver Quayde short stories. Gruber's nonfictional style is odd, more conversational than literary. He seems to be free-associating at times, and at the end he just stops, not with any kind of conclusion but with the statement, "I have also sold a substantial number of 'original' screenplays" (page 189). There is no documentation, and numerous other writers have questioned the accuracy of Gruber's memory. Countless names of people and magazines (familiar and otherwise) crop up, making the absence of an index particularly nettling.

Quibbles aside, Gruber's account is fascinating to any devotee of popular fiction generally and the pulps in particular. The fruits of his first creative spurt between 1932 and 1934 went to such wide-ranging markets as Sunday-school magazines, American Poultry Journal, service magazines (including a $1 article sale to Our Navy), and salesmanship journals. Then he went to New York and entered the pulp field, and the great names begin to flow--Arthur J. Burks, Steve Fisher, Leo Margulies, Lester Dent, F. Olin Tremaine, Cornell Woolrich, Carroll John Daly. The book is full of entertaining trivia, such as Ryerson Johnson's prowess on the musical saw. Among the more interesting chapters is one on Frederick (Heinie) Faust, better known as Max Brand. Among the general literary figures to appear are Thomas Wolfe (unfavorable) and William Lyon Phelps (favorable--he liked Gruber's work).

In some of the latter chapters, Gruber discusses the structure of mysteries and westerns and gives some advice to prospective writers. Thus, the book is part technical manual, part autobiography (though professional rather than personal), and mostly observations of a colorful time in American literary history.

46. Harper, Ralph. The World of the Thriller. Cleveland: The Press of Case Western Reserve University, 1969. xii, 139p. Notes.

In the preface to this lively and well-written academic study, Harper expresses his interest in "the existential themes of the thriller and, more particularly, in the psychology of the reader's involvement" (page viii). Though the term "thriller" covers wider ground, he is concerned almost entirely with spy novels in his discussion. While many will believe he is loading these works of entertainment with too much psychological weight, Harper makes some shrewd remarks about the development of the spy novel, how it differs from the detective story, and the influence of American hard-boiled fiction on the more recent (i. e. , since World War II) British practitioners of the form.

The volume is divided into four parts: "The Thriller: Its World," "The Thriller: Its Categories," "The Reader: His Inner World," and "The Reader: His Secret World." The authors most frequently alluded to are Eric Ambler, John Le Carré, Ian Fleming, Graham Greene, John Buchan, and (surprisingly) Raymond Chandler. Occasionally referred to are Erskine Childers, Joseph Conrad, W. Somerset Maugham, Len Deighton, Geoffrey Household, Dashiell Hammett, and Eliot West.

47. Hersey, Harold Brainerd. Pulpwood Editor: The Fabulous World of the Thriller Magazines Revealed by a Veteran Editor and Publisher. New York: Stokes, 1937. 301p. Index.

Hersey's book is unique as an account of the pulps written in their own heyday rather than through a haze of nostalgia. The early pages are spent trying to convince the reader that people of education and substance actually do read the pulps. Entertaining as the book is, it will inevitably disappoint mystery fans. The full range of pulp types is covered with relatively little on mysteries. For example, Dashiell Hammett has only one page reference in the index, Erle Stanley Gardner and Black Mask none at all.

Admittedly disliking detective fiction, Hersey makes the odd statement that it "is utterly devoid of humor and the detective heroes are the worst oafs and bullies in all popular fiction" (page 175). This statement is certainly untrue now and was (I think) equally so then. The detective story Hersey describes as disliking, though, sounds more

like the formalist stranded-house-party type than the typical
pulp variety pioneered by Daly and Hammett.

48.   Keating, H. R. F.   Murder Must Appetize (Time Re-
membered Series).   London: Lemon Tree, 1975.   63p.
Illus.

Keating's essay on the Golden Age detective story is
an avowed nostalgia piece with a good deal of critical content as well, written in the author's friendly-jokey style.
His Golden Age is compressed into the half-decade preceding
World War II.   The main essay takes up only 43 heavily-
illustrated pages.   It is followed by a section of one-paragraph
thumbnail sketches on 27 of the main practitioners.   Books
discussed at comparative length include Sayers's Murder
Must Advertise, Miles Burton's Death in the Tunnel, Nicholas
Blake's A Question of Proof, and Ngaio Marsh's Surfeit of
Lampreys.   Keating departs from his timeframe to include
postwar Edmund Crispin in the discussion.   He makes frequent reference to penciled comments written in the margin
by earlier London Library readers of some of the titles discussed.   Though hardly a book in terms of length, this is
a delightful and acute essay.

49.   Larmoth, Jeanine.   Murder on the Menu.   With recipes
by Charlotte Turgeon.   New York: Scribner's, 1972.   xv,
268p.   Index.

The first mystery-oriented cookbook concentrates on
British recipes.   The chapter headings, divided into "Murder
in the Country," "Murder in the Village," and "Murder on
the Town," are arranged more according to their mystery
elements than the usual cookbook formula of appetizers to
desserts, but the index can be used to ferret out specific
recipes.
A humorous and appreciative commentary of the classical British mystery takes up nearly as much space as the
recipes, which are presented in an easily usable format with
ingredients listed first.

50.   Mason, Bobbie Ann.   The Girl Sleuth: A Feminist
Guide.   Old Westbury, New York: The Feminist Press,
1975.   xi, 145p.

In a lively and humorous style, Mason examines the detectives in girls' series books, with an emphasis on Nancy Drew but detailed coverage of Honey Bunch, the Bobbsey Twins, and others. Though she emphasizes the importance of the self-reliant heroine to girls growing up, and its probable influence on burgeoning feminism, Mason also offers social criticism of popular fiction's reflection of its readers' prejudices, similar to Colin Watson's discussion of adult detective fiction in Snobbery with Violence (see #61). She writes, "Solving a mystery is like tidying. You can't have a perfectly laundered neighborhood as long as uncouth strangers are hanging about" (page 22).

Carolyn Keene's Nancy Drew is contrasted with Margaret Sutton's Judy Bolton, whom Mason prefers, disputing Arthur Prager's claim (see #54) that Judy is to the right of Nancy politically. Judy, whose creator, significantly, was an individual rather than a house name, bore more resemblance to a real teenage girl.

> The original Nancy Drew series, among others, values power, supremacy, conquest, property, and privilege--under the wholesome aegis of the conquest of evil. Judy Bolton books are more delicate, more attuned to individual human possibilities--the values shine through the stereotypes. The two series have different sensibilities, despite their apparent similarities [page 89].

By the way, Betsy Allen's (Betty Cavanna's) Connie Blair gets the nod as heroine of the most sexist girls' series.

51. Merry, Bruce. Anatomy of the Spy Thriller. Dublin: Gill and Macmillan, 1977. 253p. Notes, index.

An academic study that portentously declares in the introduction its adherence to the Russian Formalist school of literary criticism raises the storm signals of heavy going for most readers. For the most part, though, this is a readable and enlightening study of the structure of spy novels. Merry takes the spy novel seriously on its own terms and analyzes its plots, techniques, characters, style, and devices in depth. He traces the form to incidents in the Iliad (Ian Fleming school) and the Aeneid (John Le Carré school). He identifies four participants in the thriller: writer, reader, enemy, and agent.

Among the works given particularly detailed treatment
are Frederick Forsyth's The Day of the Jackal (with a close
examination of the plot structure), Conrad's The Secret Agent
and Under Western Eyes (compared and contrasted with modern spy fiction), and several books by Fleming, Deighton,
and Le Carré. But many writers (greats and hacks alike)
are used as examples and quoted.

Among the subjects are the differences between British
thrillers (impersonal, bachelor agent) and American thrillers
(married hero, family concerns); the language of spy fiction,
particularly its euphemisms; the traits of major characters
(agent, girl, double-agent, control); the contrast of fictional
and real-life espionage activities; the cultural pretensions
of the thriller, manifested in quotation-spouting by agents and
enemies; and the appeal of the spy novel as a modern equivalent of the epic and folktale.

There are some errors (Mickey Spillane is mistakenly
credited with "dozens of Mike Hammer books" and a few
names are misprinted), but they are relatively minor. The
most jarring note is that this learned scholar's preferred
noun for homosexual is "queer"!

52. Ousby, Ian. Bloodhounds of Heaven: The Detective in
English Fiction from Godwin to Doyle. Cambridge: Harvard
University Press, 1976. x, 194p. Illus. , notes, index.

Ousby's theme is the changing image of the fictional
detective from that of a thief-taker like Jonathan Wild,
scarcely different in the public mind from the criminals he
captured, through the middle-class police sleuth of Dickens
or Collins, made possible by the increased respectability of
the police, to Sherlock Holmes, the gifted amateur who came
to the fore when corruption charges were casting doubt on
the official police. Godwin's Caleb Williams and the translation of Vidocq's memoirs are discussed at length. This is
a highly readable scholarly contribution to literary and criminous history.

53. Palmer, Jerry. Thrillers: Genesis and Structure of
a Popular Genre. London: Edward Arnold, 1978. 232p.
Bibl. , index.

Palmer includes under the term "thriller" everything
in the crime-mystery spectrum. Thus, while the spy story
and the hardboiled are the main focus of his study, the

classical detective story is included merely as one type--a
case, comparing this with most other studies of the form,
of the tail wagging the dog. Fleming and Spillane are the
authors most frequently cited in Palmer's analysis, like
Bruce Merry's (see #51) mostly descriptive. He is generally
less impressive than Merry, though, and seems to spend
much of his space belaboring the obvious.

Palmer discusses heroes, villains, and sexuality in
his first section. He distinguishes between the "positive"
thriller (Fleming, Spillane) and the "negative" (Hammett,
Chandler, James Hadley Chase). He is hostile to the formal
detective story, claiming it "peters out somewhere around
Nero Wolfe" (page 93). Another apparent misstatement is
that Colin Watson "dislike[s] thrillers and detective stories"
(page 94). If he dislikes them, why does he write them?

Palmer includes some material on the historical roots
of the thriller in heroic romance, gothic novels (original
sense), and police memoirs and "low-life literature" and
discusses the genre theories of Northrop Frye, among others.
By the time he reaches a section called "Sociology and the
Thriller," most buffs will be ready to debark.

In sum, Palmer's is a self-important academic study
that makes some rather threadbare points in overblown lit-
crit jargon. It has some value as one of the few monographs
on the spy thriller and one of the few to discuss the "en-
forcer" stories of Don Pendleton and his imitators.

54. Prager, Arthur. Rascals at Large; or the Clue in the
Old Nostalgia. Garden City, New York: Doubleday, 1971.
334p.

Prager looks at the hardcover juvenile fiction of this
century's first half, most but not all detective stories. The
characters discussed include Tarzan, Fu Manchu (the one
ostensibly adult series covered), Nancy Drew, the Hardy
Boys, Tom Swift, Tom Slade, the Rover Boys, Jerry Todd,
Baseball Joe, Frank Merriwell, Bomba the Jungle Boy, and,
more briefly, numerous others. In contrast to the basically
serious approach of Bobbie Ann Mason to some of the same
material (see #50), this nostalgia piece is basically for fun.
The closing sentence is a memorable one: "Anyone want to
buy four hundred slightly used boys' and girls' books?"

55. Routley, Eric. The Puritan Pleasures of the Detective
Story: A Personal Monograph. London: Gollancz, 1972.
253p. Bibl. , index.

A proponent of the classical detective story in the Barzun-Taylor mold, Routley relates the form to the concept of puritanism and its roots in the values of the city. In its discussion of the genre's moral implications, the book is extremely worthwhile, and Routley offers some of the best writing extant about Chesterton's Father Brown, Ernest Bramah's Max Carrados, and H. C. Bailey's Reggie Fortune. Other writers dealt with in some detail include Conan Doyle (of course), R. Austin Freeman, Freeman Wills Crofts, John Rhode, Agatha Christie, and Dorothy L. Sayers. Many others are discussed more briefly.

While Routley offers much to celebrate, he also offers much to complain about. His British bias is unsurpassed since H. Douglas Thomson (see #7). He devotes only eleven pages to "Certain Americans," and may do that only to bring Ellery Queen (a particular favorite) into the discussion. And he is one of those all-too-plentiful commentators on the genre who rely on faulty memory and commit a long string of errors. To note a few: Hulbert Footner, not Stacy Aumonier, wrote about Madame Rosika Storey. Harry Kemelman, not Francis, writes of Rabbi Small. Gaston Leroux was not a contemporary of Gaboriau. Dupin's first name was Auguste, not Aristide.

Routley also has some highly eccentric opinions. He believes that E. C. Bentley's Trent's Last Case was the "first real detective novel" (page 120), thus dismissing The Moonstone, The Hound of the Baskervilles, and scores of others with a wave of the hand.

Routley finishes with a pessimistic word on the future of the detective story, paralleling its decline with the decline of puritanism. Though he regrets the passing of both, he believes them incapable of dealing with evil contemporary reality.

56. Ruehlmann, William. Saint with a Gun: The Unlawful American Private Eye. Foreword by Aaron Marc Stein. New York: New York University Press, 1974. xvi, 155p. Bibl.

Addressing the vigilante strain in American detection, Reuhlmann attempts to show that Philo Vance and Nero Wolfe have more in common with Mike Hammer than one might expect. He alludes to a long and varied list of sleuths--for example, Allan Pinkerton, Nick Carter, the Continental Op, Sam Spade, Philip Marlowe, Mike Shayne, Paul Pine, Peter Chambers, Shell Scott, Chester Drum--but touches on each one just long enough to fit him into the pattern of hero-as-avenger. Only Lew Archer, noted as "an interesting exception to the role of private eye as an enforcer-savior" (page 105), won't fit. There is nothing on the female private eye, however.

The final chapter deals with the slaughtering avenger of the seventies, typified by Don Pendleton's Executioner. He briefly touches on such writers as Jon Messmann and Peter McCurtin, seldom cited in other books on the genre. For a finale, Ruehlmann ties the theory into the Manson crimes and Watergate.

Though he sometimes strains to make the examples fit his theory, Ruehlmann can be an entertaining writer, as when he describes the private eye as "the American innocent gone mad" (page 129) or when he cracks about James Jones's A Touch of Danger, "Jones's debt to Hemingway practically puts the novel into receivership" (page 127).

57. Sandoe, James. The Hard-boiled Dick: A Personal Checklist. Chicago: Arthur Lovell, 1952. 9p.

This annotated list of selected private-eye fiction is without doubt the most famous nine-page pamphlet in the annals of the genre, and justly so. Expanded for inclusion in John Ball's anthology The Mystery Story (see #63), it was able to reach a much wider audience.

58. Thomas, Gilbert. How to Enjoy Detective Fiction (How to Enjoy Series). London: Rockliff, 1947. 108p. Bibl., index.

This is a hard book to locate and, frankly, not worth the trouble. By its very title, it seems wholly superfluous, an impression borne out by the contents. In its description and history of detective fiction, it is not wholly inaccurate but is as lacking in originality as any work on the genre. Short to begin with, it is padded with quotations from Poe, Conan Doyle, and other writers, plus tangential discussions of real-life crime investigation and classic criminal cases. (There is even a plea for higher wages for British police and the suggestion that the reader become a prison visitor.) Rightly or wrongly, the text suggests heavy reliance on secondary sources.

There are some careless mistakes, as usual. Melville Davisson Post is lauded for his great contribution to the detective novel, virtually nil as far as I know. To say that Sam Spade and Nick Charles are "unhampered by moral ethics" (page 43) seems wide enough of the mark to be called an error whether of fact or opinion.

The recommendation of medical, criminological, and psychological texts seems better suited to the prospective writer than the reader. The chapter on stage and film crime shows the book's attempt to cover too much and do nothing in depth--does an account of nickelodeons and D. W. Griffith belong in a book as thin as this? The final chapter gives thumbnail sketches of some of the main practitioners and lists a few of their titles. Aside from Queen, Stout, and Van Dine, all the writers listed are British, and they are a good, representative selection though the comments about them are usually rather obvious and threadbare.

59. Tuska, Jon. The Detective in Hollywood. Garden City, New York: Doubleday, 1978. xx, 436p. Illus. , index.

Tuska covers much of the same ground as William K. Everson in The Detective in Film (see #40), though from a somewhat different perspective and certainly in a different style. Where Everson stuck to the films themselves, Tuska personally interviewed many of the performers, writers, producers, directors, and others involved--and he constantly reminds the reader of the fact, quoting dialogue to show himself on a first-name basis with the stars. Where Everson maintained the role of detached observer, Tuska constantly inserts himself into the action, becomes part of the show. Where Everson was well organized and stuck to the point, Tuska constantly goes off on tangents and reveals an eye for the irrelevant detail--John Howard's model-duck collection, for example. Where Everson wrote in smooth, literate prose, Tuska is a lead-footed stylist given to unintentional humor, as in a reference to Myrna Loy's "110-pound torso." From the prologue on, Tuska's pomposity and pretension assail the reader.

Having said all this, one has to admit he does cover new ground and is consistently interesting. From the first chapter on Sherlock Holmes, it is evident that Tuska will discuss the literary origins of the movie detective stories and the lives of their authors in addition to the films themselves. Subsequent chapters deal with Philo Vance, "The Detective at Large" (covering Nero Wolfe, Bulldog Drummond, Hildegarde Withers, Miss Marple, and Perry Mason, among others), "Chinatown, My Chinatown" (about Charlie Chan,

including an interesting view of Warner Oland; Mr. Moto;
and Mr. Wong), Dashiell Hammett, The Thin Man series,
Ellery Queen (he likes the movies more than most but feels
the weakest feature of the Queen novels was the plots!!!),
The Saint and The Falcon (lumped with Queen in "The Detective in Transition"), other forties series (including The
Crime Doctor, Mike Shayne, The Lone Wolf, Dick Tracy,
The Whistler, and Boston Blackie), Raymond Chandler, film
noir, and "The Contemporary Scene," which Tuska values
far more than Everson. The last film discussed is Chinatown, featuring, of course, a chummy interview with Roman
Polanski.

　　Jon Tuska is one of the most outspoken opponents of
the convention of not giving away the ending of a mystery
story. To demonstrate this stance, he constantly gives away
endings even when there is no earthly reason to do so.

60. Usborne, Richard. Clubland Heroes. London: Constable, 1953. ix, 217p.

　　Usborne examines the mystery-adventure fiction of
Dornford Yates, John Buchan, and Sapper (H. C. McNeile).
The title comes from the fact that most of the heroes of
these books were West-End Clubmen. The vigilante tenden-
cies of these heroes are traced to the English public-school
system.
　　There is a fascinating section on Yates's choice of
names for his characters and his use of language generally.
Usborne admits that Buchan was the best writer of the three
but believes his heroes pale next to those of Yates and Sapper. He also finds Buchan's idea of competitive success
distasteful. In a footnote regarding Bulldog Drummond's
origin in novelist Gerard Fairlie, Usborne writes, "It is
amusing to think that Drummond's prototype is a writer, because one feels that Drummond could hardly sign a cheque
without making a blot and spelling his name wrong" (page
154).
　　This is basically an engaging book, though Usborne
seems more tolerant of his subjects' racism and anti-Semitism
than might seem appropriate to a present-day reader. The
lack of a checklist of books in which the various heroes appeared is unfortunate.

61. Watson, Colin. Snobbery with Violence: Crime Stories
and Their Audience. London: Eyre and Spottiswoode, 1971.

256p. Illus., index. American edition, New York: St. Martin's, 1971. 256p. Illus., index.

The author of numerous humorous detective novels, Watson presents in this volume one of the most provocative and entertaining sociological studies of crime fiction. Concentrating on the British output between the world wars, Watson exposes the class-consciousness, reactionary social ideas, and pernicious racism of much thriller and detective fiction. Among the authors targeted are E. W. Hornung, John Buchan, Edgar Wallace, H. C. McNeile (Sapper), E. Phillips Oppenheim, Leslie Charteris, Dorothy L. Sayers, Agatha Christie, and (as a more recent example) Ian Fleming. Of all Watson's horrible examples, the worst bigot by far is Sydney Horler, a writer relatively little known in the United States.

Watson chooses authors and passages that support his thesis and thus hardly gives a balanced picture. This is interesting and instructive reading for the longtime buff of mystery fiction, but I would hate to imagine anyone using it as an introduction to the field. The work is illustrated with Punch cartoons from the period. They nicely complement Watson's witty style. †

62. Amis, Kingsley. What Became of Jane Austen? and
Other Questions. London: Jonathan Cape, 1970. 223p.
American edition, New York: Harcourt Brace Jovanovich,
1971. 223p.

Among the literary essays collected here are several
related in some degree to the genre. "A New James Bond"
(pages 65-77) discusses Amis's reasons for writing Colonel
Sun--money was one--and reiterates his defense of James
Bond against his left-wing critics (see #152). In the general
discussion of genre fiction that follows, he makes the wonder-
fully bold pronouncement that "John D. MacDonald is by any
standards a better writer than Saul Bellow" (page 69). The
remarks on the process of pastiche-writing are interesting.
To the original 1968 essay are appended notes on The Man
with the Golden Gun and on Le Carré and Deighton. "Unreal
Policemen" (pages 108-125), originally a 1966 Playboy article,
discusses some famous fictional detectives, including Holmes,
Father Brown, Nero Wolfe, and Dr. Fell, all favorably contrasted with pros like Maigret and Van der Valk, tough
private eyes, and most of their amateur brethren. In a
discussion of the tough school, Amis makes the outrageous
claim that of the trio of Hammett, Chandler, and Spillane,
Spillane was the best! (page 110). Amis is surely one of
the most provocative of commentators on the mystery field,
and a whole book from him on the subject would be most
welcome. Of related interest is an essay on horror films,
"Dracula, Frankenstein, Sons, and Co." (pages 125-135).

63. Ball, John, ed. The Mystery Story. Introduction by

Martin N. Chamberlain. Del Mar: University Extension, University of California, San Diego, in cooperation with Publisher's Inc., 1976. xii, 390p. Illus., bibl.

Published in connection with the University's ambitious (and now apparently dormant) Mystery Library reprinting project, this uneven but valuable collection brought together seventeen essays on various aspects of the form, all by distinguished practitioners and scholars and all but one original to this collection.

The one exception is James Sandoe's "The Private Eye," revised and expanded from the 1952 pamphlet The Hard-boiled Dick: A Personal Checklist (see #57). The list's availability here relieves collectors (except for the most rabid first-edition types) of trying to find the very scarce original. The keen critical judgments make it an excellent reference list. Another feature with reference value is Allen J. Hubin's "Patterns in Mystery Fiction: The Durable Series Character," discussing such matters as publisher's imprints and title patterns (with lists) before embarking on a list of series characters who have appeared in five or more books. Arranged chronologically, the entries give year of debut, name of character, type (police, criminal, private, spy), country of origin, book format (paperback or hardback), number of books, and author. Leaders in the number of cases (through the end of 1975) were Nick Carter (581) and Sexton Blake (100's) among the multiauthored sleuths and Perry Mason (85) and Maigret (75) among the one-author characters. Also of reference value is Robert E. Briney's annotated list of secondary sources. (Something like the book you hold in your hand but less garrulous.)

Other contributors and subjects include Otto Penzler on amateur detectives and crooks, Michele Slung on women in detective fiction (one of the weaker chapters, surprisingly from the editor of the fine anthology Crime on Her Mind), editor Ball on ethnic detectives, Hillary Waugh on police procedurals, Donald A. Yates on locked rooms (annoyingly reticent re specific titles), Michael Gilbert on spies, Phyllis A. Whitney on gothics, and famed collector Ned Guymon on the eternal question, "Why Do We Read This Stuff?" The longest essay and one of most entertaining is Robert E. Briney's "Death Rays, Demons, and Worms Unknown to Science: The Fantastic Element in Mystery Fiction." Francis M. Nevins, Jr., contributes an informative essay on mystery pseudonyms.

Less fact-filled than the others but more thoughtful and philosophical are two excellent essays by Aaron Marc

Stein ("The Mystery Story in Cultural Perspective") and Hillary Waugh ("The Mystery Versus the Novel").

64. Barzun, Jacques, and Wendell Hertig Taylor. A Book of Prefaces to Fifty Classics of Crime Fiction, 1900-1950. New York: Garland, 1976. vi, 112p.

The authors of A Catalogue of Crime (see #10) selected fifty volumes for Garland to reprint in hardcover and wrote a short (usually two-page) introduction for each. Since many libraries either didn't need or couldn't afford the entire set, the fifty prefaces were published in separate book form in a limited edition of 250 copies. Each preface includes a brief paragraph of biography of the author or authors.
The books discussed include some very familiar titles --Chesterton's The Innocence of Father Brown, Christie's The Murder of Roger Ackroyd (they reveal the solution, effectively spoiling the fun of that one reader in a thousand who might not already know it!), Conan Doyle's The Hound of the Baskervilles, Milne's The Red House Mystery--and these are interestingly commented upon. But most readers will find more tantalizing the introductions to some of the very obscure titles the pair have unearthed--Gerald Bullett's The Jury, Thomas Kindon's Murder in the Moor, Dermot Morrah's The Mummy Case, Henry Kitchell Webster's Who Is the Next?, and Clifford Witting's Measure for Murder.

65. Borowitz, Albert. Innocence and Arsenic: Studies in Crime and Literature. New York: Harper and Row, 1977. xiv, 170p.

Most of the essays in this collection are closer to true-crime than mystery-fiction analysis. Several, though, have some genre interest. The lead essay, "The Snows on the Moors" (pages 1-25), discusses the writings about the Moors Murder Case of C. P. Snow (fictionally, in The Sleep of Reason) and his wife Pamela Hansford Johnson (factually, in On Iniquity), making interesting points about their differing approaches. Snow's early detective novel, Death Under Sail (1932), and the ways in which it foreshadows his later fiction, is the object of numerous references. Other essays discuss Robert Louis Stevenson and Dr. Jekyll and Mr. Hyde (pages 26-32) and Dickens and Edwin Drood (pages 53-62). A facetious article on the various Jack the Ripper theories (pages 87-99) includes some discussion of Mrs. Belloc Lowndes's

The Lodger and Thomas Burke's "The Hands Of Mr. Ottermole."

66. Boucher, Anthony. Multiplying Villainies: Selected Mystery Criticism, 1942-1968. Edited by Robert E. Briney and Francis M. Nevins, Jr. Foreword by Helen McCloy. Boston: Bouchercon, 1973. xii, 136p. Index.

Published in connection with the fourth annual Anthony Boucher Memorial Mystery Convention, this is the only collection to date of critical writings by the late New York Times Book Review and Ellery Queen's Mystery Magazine crime-fiction reviewer. It is the secondary source one would most like to see superseded--by a complete reprinting of Boucher's critical writings. This is only an appetizer.
Included are a twenty-page selection of Boucher's early review columns for the San Francisco Chronicle (including, among other things, a damning put-down of S. S. Van Dine and a review of Albert Camus's The Stranger in tandem with Georges Simenon's The Man Who Watched the Trains Go By); a single example (April 1949) of Boucher's short-lived stint as proprietor (succeeding Howard Haycraft) of EQMM's "Speaking of Crime" column; and (in the largest section) selections from Boucher's "Criminals at Large" columns in the Times (1951-1967), primarily his best-of-the-year summaries. Rounding out the volume are a too-short essay on Henry Kuttner's mystery fiction, an article (not previously published) on "Opera and Murder," five introductions written for the Collier Mystery Classics reprint series, and a longish review of The Annotated Sherlock Holmes, written in 1968, the year of Boucher's far-too-early death.
The editors provide author and title indexes, useful though limited to major references and omitting listings in the best-of-the-year columns.

67. Eames, Hugh. Sleuths, Inc.: Studies of Problem Solvers, Doyle, Simenon, Hammett, Ambler, Chandler. Philadelphia: Lippincott, 1978. 228p. Bibl.

Here is a nonspecialist, popular work of collective biography-criticism, a rather desultory affair that is neither very original nor very objectionable. Eames lays emphasis on the interface of real and fictional crime and includes a short note on Pat Garrett (Billy the Kid's nemesis) in addition to the five practitioners listed in the subtitle. Though interesting enough, the Garrett essay doesn't seem to fit in with the rest of the book and adds to the grab-bag feeling of the whole enterprise.

Since Eric Ambler has for some reason been written about less than the other subjects, the section on him should be the most useful. But it typifies what is in the rest of the book: a superficial and disorganized collection of facts, quotes, and plot summaries that doesn't really add up to anything illuminating. A better source on Ambler is Gavin Lambert's The Dangerous Edge (see #71), quoted by Eames.

68. Gilbert, Michael, ed., on behalf of the Crime Writers' Association. Crime in Good Company: Essays on Criminals and Crime Writing. London: Constable, 1959. x, 242p.

These fourteen essays on crime fiction sometimes take on the aspect of a technical manual, but ultimately they are more an effort to define the form and its relationship to real crime. All the contributors except for Jacques Barzun, Raymond Chandler, Stanley Ellin, and David Alexander are British, and all save Barzun, Chandler, and Eric Ambler wrote their contributions specifically for this volume.

Part one ("The Object of the Operation") has three essays on the criminal as seen by the doctor (Josephine Bell), the lawyer (Michael Underwood), and the policeman (Maurice Proctor). Though the three authors are all well-known mystery writers, the articles are straight nonfiction, with only Underwood making much reference to fictional crime.

Part two ("The General Practitioners") leads off with a longish and meaty essay on the classic detective novel by Cyril Hare, who stoutly insists that the detective story and straight fiction have strict and fixed boundaries and that the detective story can never be "literature with a capital L." The juxtaposition of Hare's narrow definition with the quite-different view advanced in Chandler's classic essay "The Simple Art of Murder" is provocative and undoubtedly calculated.

Rounding out part two, editor Gilbert advances the view that thrillers are harder to write than detective stories; Julian Symons discusses his familiar theme of the detective story and the crime novel, while decrying the greater restraints in terms of language and subject matter placed on the crime novel in comparison with general fiction at that time; and Barzun grumbles about the changes in the mystery that Symons and Chandler celebrate, placing on S. S. Van Dine the blame for introducing psychology into the detective

story. This second section, with the contributors comple-
menting and contrasting each other, is probably the most
illuminating of the three for today's reader.

Part three ("The Specialists") deals with markets
other than the novel for the crime story: L. A. G. Strong
and Stanley Ellin discuss (from different sides of the At-
lantic) the short story, followed by Roy Vickers on the stage,
Ambler on film, Mary Fitt on radio, and Alexander on television.

On the whole, this is a fine collection, well worth
seeking out for its articles by significant writers in the genre
that have not been reprinted since the book's appearance.
Gilbert's introductions to the contributors are unfailingly
witty and informative.

69.   Haycraft, Howard, ed.   The Art of the Mystery Story.
New York: Simon and Schuster, 1946. ix, 565p. Bibl.,
index.

As a follow-up to his definitive history, Murder for
Pleasure (see #1), Haycraft edited the first collection of
critical essays on the form, a milestone volume that is still
of great interest today. Though most of the essays are reprinted from other sources, a few (by Erle Stanley Gardner,
Craig Rice, and Anthony Boucher, among others) are original
to this volume.

The first section, "Mystery Matures: The Higher
Criticism," includes famous anthology introductions by Dorothy
L. Sayers, Willard Huntington Wright, and E. M. Wrong;
excerpts from the histories of H. Douglas Thomson (see #7)
and Haycraft and from Vincent Starrett's The Private Life
of Sherlock Holmes; and essays by G. K. Chesterton, R.
Austin Freeman, Marjorie Nicholson, and Joseph Wood
Krutch.

The second section, "The Rules of the Game," presents two seemingly obligatory selections, Van Dine's twenty
rules and Ronald A. Knox's decalogue, along with the partially
tongue-in-cheek Detection Club oath.

Section three, "Care and Feeding of the Whodunit,"
includes Chandler's familiar (and classic) "The Simple Art
of Murder," Dr. Fell's "Locked-Room Lecture" from John
Dickson Carr's The Three Coffins, articles on screen (Richard Mealand) and radio (Ken Crossen) mysteries, and essays
by such practitioners as Gardner, Sayers, Boucher, and
Rice.

Section four, "The Lighter Side of Crime," includes Rex Stout's famous, or notorious, exposé, "Watson Was a Woman," Christopher Ward's excruciating Philo Vance parody, "The Pink Murder Case," and two devastating swipes at the had-I-but-known school of mystery fiction: Ogden Nash's familiar "Don't Guess, Let Me Tell You" and Ben Hecht's less widely known but equally toxic parody, "The Whistling Corpse." Stephen Leacock stands out among the other humorists represented.

Section five, "Critics' Corner," gives a platform to reviewers Isaac Anderson, "Judge Lynch," Will Cuppy, and Anthony Boucher and reprints contemporary reviews of four famous mystery novels, The Moonstone, The Sign of Four, Trent's Last Case, and The Benson Murder Case, the last being Dashiell Hammett's attempted demolition of Philo Vance, who takes a terrible beating in this book. Rounding out the section are Edmund Wilson's unfriendly "Who Cares Who Killed Roger Ackroyd?," an excerpt from Nicholas Blake's introduction to the British edition of Murder for Pleasure, and Ellery Queen's "Leaves from the Editor's Notebook," some of which turned up later in the collection In the Queens' Parlor (see #82).

The sixth section, "Detective Fiction vs. Real Life," leads off with Dashiell Hammett's fascinating collection of (almost literally) one-liners, "From the Memoirs of a Private Detective"; R. Philmore's well-reasoned challenge to the science and psychology of some classic mysteries, "Inquest on Detective Stories"; and essays by J. B. White (on the law in mystery fiction) and F. Sherwood Taylor (on body disposal).

Section seven, "Putting Crime on the Shelf," presents an article on collecting mysteries by John Carter (see #37), Ellery Queen's essay on the detective short story (revised from the introduction to 101 Years' Entertainment), and James Sandoe's "Reader's Guide to Crime," a listing of mystery-fiction highspots compiled with the help of a panel of specialists and originally intended to encourage academic libraries to build representative collections of detective fiction.

The last section, "Watchman, What of the Night?," involves prophecy about the genre. Beginning with a 1905 article with the pessimistic title "The Passing of the Detective in Literature," Haycraft presents the views of Harrison R. Steeves and Philip Van Doren Stern and finishes with his own essay, "The Whodunit in World War II and After," which briefly updates Murder for Pleasure and seemingly reveals a much less conservative Haycraft than the author of that fine history, making it clear he does not share Jacques Barzun's extreme purist views.

This collection is almost as extraordinary an achievement as <u>Murder for Pleasure</u> itself. In a library that included only a dozen volumes of history and criticism of mystery fiction, this should be one of the chosen twelve.

70. Knox, Ronald A. <u>Literary Distractions</u>. London and New York: Sheed and Ward, 1958. vii, 232p.

Several of these essays and lectures make at least passing reference to mystery fiction, and two ("Father Brown" and "Detective Fiction") concern it wholly. The latter reprises Father Knox's famous decalogue of rules for detective fiction with some expansion of the accompanying comments. The chapter on the Brown stories primarily analyzes them as detective stories, not as theology.

71. Lambert, Gavin. <u>The Dangerous Edge</u>. London: Barrie and Jenkins, 1975. xv, 272p. Bibl. , index. American edition, New York: Grossman, 1976. xiii, 272p. Bibl.

Lambert's theme in this collection of biocritical essays is the traumatic events in the childhood and later lives of several writers (and one film director) that may have led them to express themselves in crime and suspense fiction. The nine subjects of the inquiry are Collins, Conan Doyle, Chesterton, Buchan, Ambler, Greene, Simenon, Chandler, and Hitchcock. The essays are unfailingly interesting. The section on Ambler may be the most valuable, primarily because he has been less frequently written about than the others.

In the section on Hitchcock, Lambert consistently ignores the literary sources of the films, giving the impression, for example, that Hitchcock was the sole guiding force behind the classic film <u>Psycho</u>, which actually followed Robert Bloch's novel rather closely.

72. Landrum, Larry N.; Pat Browne; and Ray Browne; eds. <u>Dimensions of Detective Fiction</u>. Bowling Green, Ohio: Bowling Green University Popular Press, 1976. 290p. Notes.

This collection of academic criticism and commentary includes some reprints from <u>The Armchair Detective</u>, <u>The</u>

Journal of Popular Culture, and other learned periodicals,
but most are originals. The more familiar names among
the contributors include Elliot L. Gilbert, George Grella,
and R. Jeff Banks. A few more fannish types among the
writers would have improved the general liveliness considerably.

One characteristic of academics who make one-shot
ventures into popular genres is sweeping assumptions that
reveal a lack of broad knowledge of the form. For example,
Nancy Y. Hoffman states that Anna Katharine Green's Violet
Strange was "probably the first woman detective extant"
(page 97), which is not only far from true but is amenable
to easy checking in standard references on the form. The
editors are also guilty of a certain sloppiness in not dating
reprints--Geraldine Pederson-Krag's article, reprinted from
The Psychoanalytic Quarterly, is obviously (by clues in the
text and by the 1945 cutoff date in the notes) quite an old
article, but how old is kept a secret by the editors.

In a collection of highly variable quality, Grella's
essay on the formal detective novel stands out for its style
and critical acuteness. Some writers discussed here and
rarely dealt with elsewhere include Mickey Spillane (in two
articles), John West (author of the Rocky Steele novels and
one of the rare black writers of mysteries), and Carroll
John Daly. A final section ("The Genre Extended") brings
in contributions to the mystery by writers as varied as William Faulkner (two articles) and Ishmael Reed.

73. McCleary, G. F. On Detective Fiction and Other
Things. London: Hollis and Carter, 1960. 161p. Bibl.

The first four chapters (pages 11-51) of this collection
of essays by a 93-year-old doctor-musician concern detective
fiction, and the fifth includes an examination paper on Sherlock Holmes, along with Jane Austen and Pickwick. The
first chapter is a general history and overview of the form,
agreeably written but unoriginal. The second is an appreciation of Wilkie Collins's The Moonstone, including a discussion of Sergeant Cuff's model, Inspector Whicher, and his
investigation of the Constance Kent case. The third and
fourth chapters concern Sherlock Holmes and his origins in
the detective abilities of Dr. Joseph Bell and Arthur Conan
Doyle. McCleary briefly reprises the George Edalji and
Oscar Slater cases and Conan Doyle's involvement in them.
A short Holmesian bibliography is included, and McCleary
engages in a little mocking Sherlockiana of his own.

Since the author's longevity is one of the attractions
of these graceful essays, it would have been interesting to
have the dates of the original periodical publications. The
"other things" of the title, by the way, include infant mortality,
Gilbert and Sullivan, Shaw, Stevenson, Cambridge in the
1890s, and cricket's fast bowlers.

74. Madden, David, ed. Tough Guy Writers of the Thirties.
Preface by Harry T. Moore. Carbondale: Southern Illinois
University Press, 1968. xxxix, 247p.

Among the writers discussed in this significant collection of essays on the hardboiled school are Hemingway,
Hammett, James M. Cain, John O'Hara, Horace McCoy,
Richard Hallas (Eric Knight), and Chandler. A final section
goes beyond the thirties to discuss three descendants of the
hardboiled school in detail: William Lindsay Gresham's
Nightmare Alley, John D. MacDonald's The Damned, and
Jim Thompson's The Killer Inside Me.
What makes this a good book is that most of the
critics contributing are excellent writers rather than publish-
or-perish hacks--among them, Philip Durham, Joyce Carol
Oates, Matthew J. Bruccoli, George Grella, Carolyn See,
and R. V. Cassill. But it's amusing to read in Madden's
introduction some of the high-flown excuses academics have
to trot out to justify writing about things that interest them.

75. Meet the Detective. Introduction by Cecil Madden.
London: Allen and Unwin, 1935. 142p.

Mystery writers discuss their best-known characters
in this compilation of BBC radio talks. The detectives and
criminals covered range from the world-famous--Sapper's
Bulldog Drummond, Sax Rohmer's Fu Manchu, Baroness
Orczy's The Scarlet Pimpernel, Leslie Charteris's The Saint
--to a few virtually unknown today--Rupert Grayson's Gun
Cotton, Francis D. Grierson's Professor Wells, and Andrew
Soutar's Phineas Spinnet.
The essays are uneven, of course, but the best of
them include G. D. H. and M. I. Cole on Superintendent
Wilson (surprisingly funny and in the form of a dialogue
rather than a lecture), E. C. Bentley on Philip Trent, and
Charteris on The Saint. The most puerile is Sydney Horler
on Tiger Standish, exhibiting the right-wing xenophobia discussed at length in Colin Watson's Snobbery with Violence

(see #61). Approaches differ. Anthony Wynne on Dr. Eustace Hailey strikes one as a commercial for the series. Sapper on Drummond goes for the light touch of an after-dinner speech. Some (like A. E. W. Mason on Hanaud) seem to be giving a genuine account of the genesis of the character in question. Orczy on The Pimpernel (a surprising inclusion here) is rather florid and not too informative.

Others discussed include Freeman Wills Crofts's French, H. C. Bailey's Mr. Fortune, and R. Austin Freeman's Dr. Thorndyke.

Overall, the book is not as interesting as one suspects it should be, certainly less so than Otto Penzler's similar collection (see #81) of forty-plus years later, perhaps because of the sameness of the format the authors had to fit into and the impulses of some of them to do advertising copy (most inappropriate on the BBC) rather than analysis.

76. Mystery and Detection Annual 1972. Beverly Hills, California: Donald Adams, 1972. x, 264p. Illus.

77. Mystery and Detection Annual 1973. Beverly Hills, California: Donald Adams, 1973. x, 337p. Illus.

This annual collection of essays, notes, and reviews, edited and published by an Occidental College English professor, was a top class production in every way, and its short run of only two years truly regrettable.

The 1972 volume includes several articles on Poe, an essay on Ross Macdonald's eye imagery, mystery-related poetry (by J. E. Harrison, Edward Lauterbach, Ann Stanford, W. B. Vasels, and Paul Bowles), and articles on Jacques Futrelle, R. Austin Freeman, Edgar Wallace (a reminiscence by his daughter), Horace McCoy, Gertrude Stein, and Dashiell Hammett, among others. Perhaps most interesting, however, is the book-review section, in which Julian Symons reviews Barzun and Taylor's A Catalogue of Crime (see #10), Wilbur Jordan Smith laments the poor coverage of nineteenth-century detective fiction in Hagen's Who Done It? (see #16), and famed collector E. T. (Ned) Guymon, Jr., celebrated Tage La Cour and Harald Mogensen's The Murder Book (see #102), among other reviews of primary and secondary sources.

The 1973 volume focuses on the Southern California detective story, with essays on Chandler and Macdonald and a previously unpublished pulp novelette by McCoy. Wilbur Jordan Smith expands on his contention that Hagen left out a good deal of nineteenth-century detective fiction. Mystery writers Julian Symons and Ngaio Marsh offer reminiscences. Ann Stanford continues "The Mystery Poem," begun in the first annual. There is an interview with Simenon, and other essays discuss Poe, William Godwin, Jr., Paul Bowles, and Dorothy L. Sayers.

Though many of the contributions have an academic sound to them, the editor has ensured a preponderance of lively writing, and the second volume remains a beautiful production in all particulars.

78. Nevins, Francis M., Jr. The Mystery Writer's Art. Bowling Green, Ohio: Bowling Green University Popular Press, 1970. xii, 338p. Bibl.

Aside from Haycraft's The Art of the Mystery Story (see #69), this is the best general collection of critical essays on detective fiction.

Part I, "Appreciations," deals with individual writers and films. In the first of two articles on Poe, Robert A. W. Lowndes gives perhaps the fullest summary to appear in print of the innovations (and traditions-to-be) found in Poe's Dupin stories. J. R. Christopher also discusses the Poe tradition and contributes a useful annotated bibliography of books and articles on Poe's detective fiction. Ellery Queen's (i.e., Frederic Dannay's) oft-reprinted essay about his boyhood discovery of Sherlock Holmes comes next, followed by Robert E. Briney on Sax Rohmer, a longish and excellent essay; Norman Donaldson on R. Austin Freeman, reprinted from his biography of Freeman (see #166); Charles Shibuk on Henry Wade; Robert I. Edenbaum on Hammett; editor Nevins on the four Drury Lane novels (by Ellery Queen under the name Barnaby Ross), reprinted from Royal Bloodline (see #201); Frank E. Robbins on A. A. Fair's (Erle Stanley Gardner's) Donald Lam and Bertha Cool; Robin Wood on Hitchcock's Psycho--ignoring, like so many commentators, the contribution of novelist Robert Bloch; Ronald Richie on High and Low, a Japanese film adaptation of an Ed McBain novel; and William K. Everson on "Six Mystery Movies and their Directors."

Part II, "Taxonomy," features more generalized discussions, including Philip Durham on the Black Mask school, reprinted from Madden's Tough Guy Writers of the Thirties (see #74); John Dickson Carr's "The Grandest Game in the World," an essay on the classical form originally written as an introduction to a collection of the ten greatest detective

novels (never published); Jacques Barzun's introduction to
the anthology The Delights of Detection, an expression of
his usual purist theme; Frank D. McSherry, Jr., on "The
Janus Resolution," about mysteries with indeterminate occult
content; and Donald A. Yates on locked-room mysteries,
similar but not identical to his contribution to John Ball's
The Mystery Story (see #63).
   Part III, "Speculation and Critique," includes essays
by Elliot L. Gilbert ("The Detective as Metaphor in the Nine-
teenth Century"), Ross Macdonald ("The Writer as Detective
Hero"), and William O. Aydelotte ("The Detective Story as
a Historical Source"), and the second contribution of Mc-
Sherry (on science-fictional mysteries).

79. Overton, Grant. Cargoes for Crusoes. New York:
Appleton, 1924. x, 416p. Illus., bibl., index.

   Actually copublished by three major companies of the
day (George H. Doran and Little, Brown, in addition to
Appleton), this collection of essays on popular writers seems
more an advertising medium than a critical study--there is
even a current price list on the works of the writers discussed. Mystery practitioners included are Melville Davisson Post, E. Phillips Oppenheim, and Frank L. Packard.
A few of the other subjects--Jeffrey Farnol, Aldous Huxley,
Michael Arlen, and Courtney Riley Cooper--occasionally
touched on the mystery field. Each essay includes a chronological list of the author's books and a reference to sources
of further information.

80. Panek, LeRoy. Watteau's Shepherds: The Detective
Novel in Britain, 1914-1940. Bowling Green, Ohio: Bowling
Green University Popular Press, 1979. 232p. Index, notes.

   The stated purpose of this book is to go beyond the
criticism of the detective novel as puzzle to a broader and
more literary examination. After an introductory chapter,
eight writers are discussed in some detail: E. C. Bentley,
Agatha Christie, A. A. Milne, Dorothy L. Sayers, Anthony
Berkeley Cox, Margery Allingham, John Dickson Carr, and
Ngaio Marsh. The title comes from Robert Graves and Alan
Hodge's The Long Week-End: "Detective novels, however,
were no more to be judged by realistic standards than one
would judge Watteau's shepherds and shepherdesses in terms
of contemporary sheep-farming."

Perceiving the roots of the detective story as much in nineteenth-century adventure fiction as in the works of Poe, Gaboriau, and Conan Doyle, Panek sees Golden Age detection as a reaction to the adventure thrillers of such writers as Wallace, Oppenheim, and Rohmer, who had borrowed a detective interest from Doyle. He compares the Golden Age detective story's structure, rather convincingly, with that of a joke.

Always stimulating, Panek puts forth some opinions that will draw hearty objection. For example, he seems to underrate Christie as a writer and puzzle-maker, implying quite wrongly that she does not play fair with the reader in her least-likely-person whodunits. More than anyone save Queen and Carr, Christie always provides the clues. And is it true, as Panek claims, that any of the characters in And Then There Were None could have feigned death and been revealed as the murderer?

Though denying Sayers her middle initial, which would have won him her undying enmity, Panek offers a better critical summary of her detective novels than most, perhaps any, of the monographs about her work. The chapter on Cox (who wrote as Anthony Berkeley and Francis Iles) is one of the more interesting surveys, concerning a writer surprisingly little reprinted and little written about today. The excellent chapter on Allingham makes me want to rediscover a writer who has never been a favorite of mine.

An appendix discusses detective plots in detail, even including a set of flow charts.

This book is one of the best ever written on the formal detective story. Panek is a rare critic in his ability to discuss a mystery in all its aspects--plot, character, theme--usually without revealing solutions. He can make tantalizing points and comments about a book without examining it to the point of overkill and consequent boredom.

81. Penzler, Otto, ed. The Great Detectives. Boston: Little, Brown, 1978. xvii, 281p. Bibl.

Twenty-six writers of detective fiction discuss their series sleuths in this entertaining collection, similar to (but much more varied and interesting than) the 1935 BBC collection, Meet the Detective (see #75).

Approaches, of course, vary. H. R. F. Keating's funny piece on Inspector Ghote takes the form of the views of a colleague in the Bombay Crime Branch. Ngaio Marsh on Roderick Alleyn and Michael Innes on John Appleby tell

us exactly where and in what circumstances their sleuths
were first written about. Christianna Brand identifies her
father-in-law as the real-life model for Inspector Cockrill.
In the manner of a Sherlockian, Robert L. Fish writes of
his Captain José Da Silva as a real person. Ed McBain
reveals his original intention to kill off the 87th Precinct's
Steve Carella at the end of The Pusher, third book in the
series. In one of the best essays, Baynard Kendrick describes his meeting with the blinded World War I veteran who
became the model for Captain Duncan Maclain. Adam Hall
does a thumbnail sketch of Quiller with no reference to the
circumstances of his creation. In journalistic style, John
Ball interviews Virgil Tibbs over lunch.

Among the other characters covered are Ross Macdonald's Lew Archer, Donald Hamilton's Matt Helm, Richard
Lockridge's Mr. and Mrs. North, and Nicolas Freeling's
Van der Valk. A few surprising inclusions turn up--a juvenile (Carolyn Keene's Nancy Drew), a one-shot (Vera Caspary's Mark McPherson), and a comic strip (Chester Gould's
Dick Tracy).

Editor Penzler introduces each chapter and provides
a bibliography/filmography.

82. Queen, Ellery (Frederic Dannay and Manfred B. Lee).
In the Queens' Parlor and Other Leaves from the Editors'
Notebook. New York: Simon and Schuster, 1957. ix,
195p. Index.

Most of the brief (usually one- or two-page) entries
in this highly entertaining miscellany are reprinted or adapted
from story introductions in Ellery Queen's Mystery Magazine,
which in the forties and fifties were often a vehicle for editorial commentary on all sorts of criminous matters.

Some of subjects covered include notable presentation
copies of books of detective fiction, methods of choosing
pseudonyms (including the origin of Ellery Queen), "Desert
Island Reading" (examining various "best" lists, including
Queen's poll of experts to select the "Golden Dozen" best
detective short stories), the famous nostalgic account of
Frederic Dannay's first boyhood encounter with Sherlock
Holmes (a part of the introduction to the editors' suppressed
anthology, The Misadventures of Sherlock Holmes), title
patterns in mystery novels, and Stuart Palmer's penguin
trademark.

Reading Queen story intros has some of the compulsive
quality of eating peanuts. The absence here of the stories
being introduced is rarely a serious annoyance.

83. Sayers, Dorothy L. Unpopular Opinions. London:
Gollancz, 1946. 190p.

Sayers's essay collection is divided into the theological,
the political, and the critical. The last section (pages 134-
190) is the one that concerns us, dealing entirely with detective fiction and almost entirely with Sherlock Holmes.
The Sherlockian studies concern Holmes's college career,
Dr. Watson's Christian name, his widowerhood, and the
dates in "The Red-Headed League." They are joined by the
famous (and frequently reprinted) essay "Aristotle on Detective
Fiction." Needless to say, Sayers could perpetrate Sherlockian pseudoscholarship with the best of them. As she
points out in her foreword, "The rule of the game is that
it must be played as solemnly as a county cricket match at
Lord's: the slightest touch of extravagance or burlesque
ruins the atmosphere" (page 9).

84. Stewart, A. W. Alias J. J. Connington. London:
Hollis and Carter, 1947. xi, 279p.

The main claim this mixed collection of historical,
literary, and scientific essays has to inclusion here is that
its chemistry-professor author used his mystery-writing
nom de plume to help sell the book. The preface tells the
origins of the name J. J. Connington and discusses aliases
and pseudonyms generally. Stewart also compares the work
of the scientist and the detective novelist--the main parallel
(unsurprisingly) is that both require a logical mind. An
article called "Where Plots Come From" (pages 25-39) is
a general literary essay but draws many examples from
mystery fiction--for example, works of Poe, Conan Doyle,
Belloc-Lowndes, and Stevenson. Of related but nonfictional
interest are a fact-crime essay and a discussion of the Loch
Ness monster and other mysterious phenomena.

85. Wilson, Edmund. Classics and Commercials: A Literary Chronicle of the Forties. New York: Farrar, Straus,
1950. x, 534p.

Though most of this collection of critical articles has
nothing to do with the matter at hand, it is included here
for Wilson's famous trio of essays debunking detective fiction: "Why Do People Read Detective Stories?" (pages 231-
237), "Who Cares Who Killed Roger Ackroyd?" (pages 257-

265), and "Mr. Holmes, They Were the Footprints of a Giant Hound" (pages 266-274). Articles of related interest include "A Treatise on Tales of Horror" (pages 172-181), and the part of "The Boys in the Back Room" that concerns James M. Cain (pages 19-22).

Much as I disagree with his views, I confess to finding Wilson's attacks more stimulating than infuriating. He makes some interesting points. " ... I began to nurse a rankling conviction that detective stories in general are able to profit by an unfair advantage in the code which forbids the reviewer to give away the secret to the public--a custom which results in the concealment of the pointlessness of a good deal of this fiction and affords a protection to the authors which no other department of writing enjoys" (page 233). Having said that, Wilson dutifully observes the code and does not reveal endings, as least in the first of the three articles. In his general condemnation, he has faint praise for Stout, Carr, and Chandler, and nearly unalloyed scorn for Sayers, Hammett, Marsh, Allingham, and Christie (though he does admit the ending of Death Comes as the End surprised him). Conan Doyle he likes.   †

86. Block, Lawrence. Writing the Novel: From Plot to Print. Cincinnati: Writer's Digest Books, 1979. 197p.

Although Block does not confine himself to the mystery-suspense field in this highly readable manual, most of his own work falls into that category and many of the examples he uses are drawn from crime fiction. Carrying the reader step by step through the process of preparing to write, writing, and marketing a novel, Block offers no easy answers and stresses that no two writers will achieve their aims in exactly the same way. He does, however, provide some very clear and sane advice and gives heart to struggling authors by an honest admission of his own missteps, including starting books and never finishing them and finishing books and never managing to sell them. In the course of the book, Block reveals quite a bit about the development of the novel The Burglar Who Liked to Quote Kipling, which he was working on at the same time as this manual. The smooth finished product shows no indication of the problems and setbacks he encountered while writing it.

This is such an entertaining piece of writing, it could be enjoyed by fans of Block's other books even if writing a novel were the farthest thing from their minds.

87. Burack, A. S. , ed. Writing Detective and Mystery Fiction. Boston: The Writer, 1945. x, 237p.

Leading off with Dorothy L. Sayers's 46-page historical essay, "Detective Fiction: Origins and Development," from the introduction to her famous anthology Omnibus of

Crime, this collection presents 25 more essays, mostly by practitioners, advising the novice mystery writer. Among them is S. S. Van Dine's "Twenty Rules for Writing Detective Stories," of historical interest but pretty well outmoded by 1945. Burack included the essay because at least five other contributors made reference to it. Howard Haycraft's essay on "The Rules of the Game" is reprinted from Murder for Pleasure (see #1). Most of the other articles are from The Writer magazine.

The contributors include some whose names are still well known in the field--Q. Patrick (Patrick Quentin), A. A. Fair (Erle Stanley Gardner), Richard Lockridge, Van Wyck Mason, Dorothy B. Hughes, George Harmon Coxe--and others who have lapsed into relative obscurity--Clyde B. Clason, Todd Downing, Kurt Steel, Cortland Fitzsimmons. Though most are entertainingly written, the essays vary in their helpfulness. Coxe's article seems a particularly sincere and practical effort to aid the newcomer. Patrick entertainingly lampoons Van Dine and opts for no rules at all in the writing of mystery fiction, other than "those which govern good fiction of any kind" (page 67). Though much of the advice is good and undated, the essays may have more value in shedding light on the works of their authors than in instructing the novice, who is probably better served by more recent manuals.

Oddly, the book has practically nothing to say about the economics of mystery writing, descriptions of which in Haycraft and Rodell (see #97) must have proved discouraging to many aspiring mystery writers of the forties, though they didn't scare off the good ones.

88. Burack, A. S. , ed. Writing Suspense and Mystery Fiction. Boston: The Writer, 1977. ix, 341p.

Although a few historical essays--by Sayers, Van Dine, and Haycraft--and one poem (Ogden Nash's "Don't Guess, Let Me Tell You") are repeated from Burack's earlier collection (see #87), this is a new book rather than a new edition. Of the thirty how-to articles in the main section, only one (by A. A. Fair) was in the earlier collection. Contributors include such present-day practitioners as Stanley Ellin, Joe Gores, Edward D. Hoch, Ngaio Marsh, Joyce Porter, Bill Pronzini, Michael Underwood, Phyllis A. Whitney, and Collin Wilcox. A chapter on "Casual Notes on the Mystery Novel" is reprinted from Raymond Chandler Speaking (see #119). The final two chapters, "A Layman's Guide to Law and the Courts" and "Glossary of Legal Terms," are

reprinted from the American Bar Association's pamphlet
Law and the Courts.
    As with the earlier volume, the discussions are strictly
literary rather than commercial.

89.   Highsmith, Patricia.   Plotting and Writing Suspense
Fiction. Boston: The Writer, 1966.   149p.   Reprinted with
new introduction, 1972.   viii, 149p.

    Highsmith conveys an overall attitude toward writing
and the arts generally, rather than producing a nuts-and-
bolts writer's manual.   As such, the book may be more useful for its insights into Highsmith's own writings than as a
how-to work.   Highsmith seems to resent the suspense label,
along with any categorization that restricts the writer's im-
agination and options.   "My advice to young and beginning
writers, if they wish to stay free agents, is to keep as clear
of the suspense label as possible" (page 142).
    Most of the author's examples are drawn from her
own work, for she claims to read very few suspense novels
by other people.   When she does use others as examples,
they are classy ones indeed--Julian Symons and Graham
Greene in novels and Vincent Starrett, Borden Deal, and
Cornell Woolrich in short stories.   In a very personal style,
she discusses many rejections, setbacks and rough spots
from her own career.   One interesting revelation is that
more than half of her short stories do not sell.   One topic
discussed here (and usually not in other sources) is the process of abridging a novel for magazine publication.
    Highsmith includes a detailed description of the plotting,
writing, and selling of her novel The Glass Cell.

90.   Hogarth, Basil.   Writing Thrillers for Profit (The
Writers' and Artists' Library, Vol. VI).   London: A. and
C. Black, 1936.   xii, 158p.

    Of the three technical manuals on mystery fiction
published in 1936, this is easily the best known.   Hogarth
includes under thrillers all the variants of the mystery and
crime novel, but his emphasis is almost entirely on the pure
detective story, and his approach is very nuts-and-bolts-ish.
The advice given is conventional and unsurprising but well
expressed and probably quite helpful to a beginning mystery
writer of the time.   Obviously, its value now is more as
history than as a guide for writers in a field that has changed

considerably, for good or ill, but many of the general points
(if not the specific examples) are still valid today.

Hogarth apparently used a questionnaire of writers in
the field to bolster his arguments. The writers quoted include the well known--John Rhode, Anthony Berkeley, Stuart
Palmer, John Dickson Carr--as well as the forgotten--Sid
G. Hedges, Leslie Despard, Roger East, Firth Erskine,
Neville Brand. An extraordinary number of the books cited
are totally unfamiliar today.

A comment regarding the love interest in detective
fiction illustrates both Hogarth's traditionalist views and his
sense of humor: "The love interest, therefore, plays the
same function in a detective novel as a wireless set in modern households; less for its intrinsic importance than because
it supplies an amiable background when all else fails" (page
40).

C. Daly King is Hogarth's special whipping boy, first
charged with being too intellectual, then with faulty science,
then with overdoing the use of maps. Hogarth generally does
not favor the American detective story, but he does include
Queen, Gardner, Van Dine, and Palmer among his favorite
examples. Unsurprisingly, Dashiell Hammett and Carroll
John Daly are never mentioned.

For reasons of historical interest, it is unfortunate
that Hogarth says nothing about agents, contracts, advances,
manuscript preparation, or the mechanics of marketing a
novel, matters most writers' manuals of today do consider.
He does go into some practical matters of real-life crime
detection, though, making a very good point on the inefficacy
of fingerprints. Writers of mystery fiction since do not
seem to have followed his advice, though, as they still think
any surface can bring forth multiple identifiable fingerprints.

Nigel Morland, one of Hogarth's competitors in the
how-to field (see #92), is miscalled "Marsland" here, a
careless error probably based on the illegibility of some-
body's handwriting. Finally, Hogarth has the annoying habit
of using unattributed quotations for no apparent reason.

91. Koontz, Dean R. Writing Popular Fiction. Cincinnati:
Writer's Digest Books, 1972. 232p. Index.

Koontz, who began his career as a science-fiction
writer and lately has worked mostly in the crime-suspense
field, deals with seven fictional categories here, of which
three (suspense, mysteries, and gothic-romance) are related
to the subject at hand. The others are science fiction,

fantasy, westerns, and erotica. The opening chapter title, "Hammer, Nails, and Wood," tips the reader off that this is the ultimate nuts-and-bolts writer's manual, as far as could be imagined from the aesthetic discussions of High-smith (see #89). Very frankly and specifically, Koontz out-lines his tricks and methods for successful reader manipu-lation. In his defense of "category" versus "mainstream" fiction, Koontz identifies as category writers Homer (adven-ture-fantasy), Poe (fantasy and mystery), and Mark Twain (ad-venture-suspense). Unlike some how-to writers, Koontz con-stantly uses examples, both from his own work and others'.

Though some will probably consider the approach overly mechanical, this book is full of practical and useful advice, now only somewhat dated. (For example, the market for gothics is not what it was at the time Koontz was writ-ing.) Koontz does not ignore the practical and marketing aspects of writing, devoting his last two chapters to some very helpful information in these areas, discussing what class postage to use, whether to have letterhead stationery, how and when to get an agent, and even getting into tax deductions for writers and whether writers should flee to Ireland.

92. Morland, Nigel. How to Write Detective Novels (Prac-tical Handbook Series, No. 32). London: Allen and Unwin, 1936. 74p. Bibl.

From the start, Morland stresses that detective fiction, with its demands of logical construction, is more difficult to write than ordinary novels. "Indeed, if 'genius is the infinite capacity for taking pains,' the finest detective books are works of almost transcendental genius!" (page 16). He advises the analytical study of many detective novels, stress-ing the opportunities for individuality of treatment within the general guidelines but discouraging too much experimentation by beginners. He also stresses the importance of expert specialized knowledge of medicine, jurisprudence, and crimi-nology. He divides the field into three types: pure detection (Poe, Van Dine, Freeman), sheer thriller (outside the scope of his discussion, involving no detection save by luck or intuition), and the mixed type, into which the bulk of detective fiction falls, though the mixture of the elements varies from author to author.

Always practical rather than inspirational, Morland stresses character biographies, maps and plans, and lays down some absolute rules that many writers have broken: that the plot must be worked out in detail before the writing begins, that the detective cannot be the narrator. There is a good section on scientific error, advising the checking and rechecking of all facts (and not just from printed sources). The recommended reading sticks to legal and criminological titles, rather than fiction, and Morland's reference to specific authors and titles is sparser than in most books of this type. He refers to his own work only glancingly, though references to his mentor, Edgar Wallace, are frequent. As with most early technical manuals, there is no discussion of marketing the novel.

Morland's advice is mostly good, though basically applicable to the classical form and in some respects outmoded today.

93. Murder Manual: A Handbook for Mystery Story Writers. Introduction by H. F. Wight. East San Diego, California: The Wight House, 1936. 120p.

Of the three manuals published in 1936, this is the only one of American origin. It is also much the poorest, full of simplistic statements and doubtful information. The stated aim is to provide a source of data for mystery writers, with material on story construction seemingly included as an afterthought.

Part I, on medical aspects and murder methods, is credited to Irene E. Young, RN. Part II covers "the mental angle," hypnotism (an apparently ill-informed article by one Jesse Kaye, who claims that only one person in six can be hypnotized and that a subject can be hypnotized to commit an act against his or her normal inclinations, including murder), as well as locale, characters, plots, clues, humor, and pace. The main message of these chapters seems to be that all this stuff should be in the story. For help in how to put it in, a writer would be well advised to look elsewhere.

References to published mysteries are practically nonexistent here, and there is no recognizable name connected with the project. The book is hard to come by, and while it is included here for the sake of completeness, I can't think of a reason for anyone else to seek it out.

94. Mystery Writers of America. The Mystery Writer's Handbook. Edited by Herbert Brean. New York: Harper, 1956. xx, 268p. Bibl.

Beginning with Anthony Boucher's analysis of the kinds of mysteries being published in the mid-fifties, the volume

moves on to articles by various hands on the subject of
mystery technique. A running commentary by editor Brean
links the articles. There are also four chapters in which
writers give their answers to a questionnaire about their
working habits, including "How to Start a Story," "When I
Write," "The Biggest Stumbling Blocks," and "The Best
Tricks of the Mystery Trade."

The long list of contributors includes some of the
biggest names, then and now, in the genre--for example,
Michael Gilbert, John D. MacDonald, Rex Stout, John Dickson Carr, Margery Allingham, John Creasey--and others
whose names might be almost totally unfamiliar today--Perry
D. Westbrook, Emma Lou Fetta, Austin F. Roberts, Sidney
Porcelain, Malden Grange Bishop, Clayre and Michael Lip-
man. At least one of the contributors, Samm Sinclair Baker,
has become a bestselling writer in fields far removed from
detective fiction. The biographical section at the beginning
lists 32 contributors.

A special feature, for readers and collectors as much
as for aspiring writers, is an updated version of the Howard
Haycraft-Ellery Queen Library of Detective-Crime-Mystery
Fiction, a listing of the genre's highspots to that date and
still a most worthwhile reading list.

While much of the advice (on plotting, story structure,
characterization) is as valuable today as the day it was written, some of it is inevitably dated. Robert Arthur, writing
on radio mysteries, admits to the takeover by television but
says that the listener "can find a radio mystery being broad-
cast almost any hour of the day or night" (page 194). If
only that were true today!

Unlike some earlier manuals, this one does include
information on the economics of mystery writing, slightly
more encouraging than earlier accounts by Haycraft (see #1)
and Rodell (see #97), as well as advice on dealing with
agents, contracts, publishers, reviews, and other matters.

95. Mystery Writers of America. Mystery Writer's Handbook. Newly revised edition. Edited by Lawrence Treat.
Cincinnati: Writer's Digest Books, 1976. 275p.

The second edition is virtually a new work, though
it follows the format of its predecessor and recycles a few
articles from the first edition (by Fredric Brown, Pauline
Bloom, Hillary Waugh, Dana Lyon, Barbara Frost, John D.
MacDonald, Rex Stout, Margery Allingham, and Carl D.
Hodges). Again, there are questions to which several writers

respond: "Why Do You Write?," "Where Do You Get Your
Ideas?," "When and How Do You Write?," "Avoiding Clichés
Like the Plague," "How Do You Handle Stumbling Blocks?,"
and "Tricks of the Trade." In an early chapter, Bruce Cassiday updates Anthony Boucher's categorization from the
earlier volume. Perhaps because today's mysteries are a
good deal harder to pigeonhole, Cassiday's taxonomy makes
quite a bit less sense than Boucher's.

While there are good chapters here--Aaron Marc
Stein's practical essay on style is an example--this is generally not nearly as useful a book as its predecessor.

96. Nixon, Joan Lowery. Writing Mysteries for Young
People. Boston: The Writer, 1977. xi, 123p.

This useful if unscintillating how-to manual on juvenile
mystery novels is the only one of its kind to my knowledge,
though juvenile (and adult) mystery writer Phyllis A. Whitney
covers the mystery among other types in her Writing Juvenile
Stories and Novels. Nixon won the Mystery Writers of America Edgar award for best juvenile mystery of 1979 with The
Kidnapping of Christina Lattimore.

97. Rodell, Marie F. Mystery Fiction: Theory and Technique. Introduction by John W. Vandercook. New York:
Duell, Sloan and Pearce, 1943. x, 230p. Bibl.

The work of a longtime editor of mysteries (who wrote
some herself as Marion Randolph), this volume has long been
regarded as one of the basic instructional manuals for mystery writers. As did Carolyn Wells before her (see #99),
Rodell invokes the current President (F. D. R. this time) to
exemplify the readers of stature that mystery fiction attracts.
The book takes a more restrictive approach to characters,
clues, and plot devices than a similar volume might today
with the new freedoms offered by the form. And Rodell
draws a clear line between straight fiction (literature) and
mystery fiction (product). Though she makes an occasional
nod toward the horror novel and mystery-adventure (basically
spy) novel, her main focus is the bread-and-butter whodunit.

Much of the technical advice is still valid. Some of
the other sections are more interesting for their historical
value. The chapter on taboos of the mystery novel as of
1943 includes many sex-related proscriptions that do not
exist today. The economic section makes a chilling state-

ment: "The average mystery writer makes from the sale of his book no more than five hundred dollars" (page 213). Reprint rights from the fledgling paperback industry might bring in an extra $150 (page 217).

Rodell includes a three-page reading and reference list and appendixes on publishers' contracts, proofreading symbols, and the steps of a work from manuscript to book form.

98. Turner, Robert. Some of My Best Friends Are Writers, But I Wouldn't Want My Daughter to Marry One. Los Angeles: Sherbourne, 1970. 253p.

Somewhere between a how-to manual and a memoir, this account by a veteran magazine writer and paperback novelist is one of the most entertaining and honest accounts of the commercial writing life ever penned. Turner, who claimed to have contributed to more periodicals than any other writer, did it all and saw it all in a career that included agenting, TV scripting, comic-book continuity writing, an erotic-satirical novel for Maurice Girodias's Olympia Press, novelizations of the TV show Wagon Train, ghost-writing (for comedian Ken Murray among others), paperback suspense novels in the old Ace-Double format, and an endless flow of short stories for the pulps, the slicks, and the digest-sized mystery magazines. He has interesting observations to make about all these activities, as well as hard-headed advice for the novice.

Turner touches on subjects that other how-to-write oracles steer clear of, such as the use of drugs and alcohol to stimulate writing. (He doesn't advise it.) He also advises on what typewriter to buy, what to do about sex while writing, and others matters most writing teachers just don't get around to.

99. Wells, Carolyn. The Technique of the Mystery Story (The Writer's Library). Introduction by J. Berg Esenwein. Springfield, Massachusetts: The Home Correspondence School, 1913. xiv, 336p. Index. Revised edition, 1929. xiv, 435p. Illus., index.

Besides being the first how-to of the detective story, this pioneering volume is probably the first book of any kind wholly devoted to the form. Though Wells briefly discusses ghost and riddle stories, her primary focus is on the pure detective story as it existed before World War I.

Wells strikes many notes that would be repeated in later studies down to the present day: the appeal of puzzle-solving, the nonrecognition of detective stories as serious literature, the numbers of eminent citizens (notably President Woodrow Wilson) who enjoy detective fiction. While it would be a mistake to suggest that any new writer in the form (even one drawn to period settings) use this volume as a handbook, the fact remains that many of the points Wells makes about plotting are equally valid today. This book probably made a greater contribution to detective fiction than its author's enjoyable but sometimes inept novels.

Wells does much quoting, both from works of mystery fiction and commentaries, but she chooses her sources well: Poe, Conan Doyle, Henry James, Brander Matthews, Robert Louis Stevenson. Perhaps, as in her anthologies of verse, Wells's greatest talent was as a compiler rather than a writer. As in her memoirs (see #231), the organization sometimes seems a bit casual, but she almost always has something worthwhile to say.

The volume's greatest value is its historical interest, its discussion of and quotations from such forgotten practitioners as Francis Lynde, Harrison J. Holt, Frederick Trevor Hill, and A. Maynard Barbour. The writers most frequently alluded to are the expected ones: Poe, Conan Doyle, Gaboriau, Green, Collins, Leroux.

Readers have often wondered why Wells, a humorist herself and a noted collector and appreciator of humor, never showed much in her detective fiction. She says here, "If romance is out of place in a detective story, humor is even more so.... The best Detective Stories are absolutely void of it, and except in the hands of a whimsical genius it is entirely out of place" (page 300). Israel Zangwill is advanced as the rule-proving exception. Am I alone in thinking that a little comedy would not have hurt the Fleming Stone novels?

A view of the publishing scene in 1913 would have added to the fascination of this work, but Wells gives absolutely no attention to the marketing of a mystery. Her concerns are strictly literary. †

100. Haining, Peter. Mystery! An Illustrated History of
Crime and Detective Fiction. Designed by Christopher Scott.
London: Pictorial Presentations/Souvenir Press, 1977.
176p. Illus.

Very much along the lines of The Murder Book (see
#102), this is even more devoted to illustrations and even
less to narrative text. Haining is concerned strictly with
story illustration, especially magazine covers and interior
art, as opposed to photographs of authors or stills from
films and plays. He begins with the Newgate Calendar and
finishes at the beginning of World War II, after which few
detective stories have been illustrated apart from the dust
jacket.
Some of the illustrations are in color. As might be
expected, dime novels, pulp magazines, and comics loom
rather larger here than in other histories.
The text is slight in both its length and (sometimes)
its grasp of the facts. Where did Haining get the idea that
the three most famous fictional detectives were Dupin, Holmes,
and Father Brown (page 96)? Did Dime Detective publish
"heavily-erotic" stories? (Spicy Detective maybe.) Michael
Dred is misspelled "Dread." In the biggest whopper of the
lot, Haining says The Murder of Roger Ackroyd was Agatha
Christie's first novel! Roger Sheringham, described here
as "likeable," has generally been considered anything but.
One illustration is identified with a 1938 story by John D.
MacDonald, several years before his actual debut.
Shaky as it is on details, this book is well worth
perusing for its pictures. It is, though, both more limited
and less impressive overall than The Murder Book.

101. Keating, H. R. F. , ed. Crime Writers: Reflections on Crime Fiction. London: British Broadcasting Corporation, 1978. 160p. Illus. , bibl. , index.

Loosely based on (and expanded from) a BBC television series, this worthwhile collection offers seven essays by crime writers and critics with a historical introduction and linking material between chapters by Mike Pavett. Reginald Hill, in a thoughtful essay on Conan Doyle, deals with the Sherlock Holmes stories in a historical and literary rather than a Sherlockian context--he regards the more detailed biographies of Holmes as "religious rather than critical" (page 22), a telling phrase. Colin Watson writes on the Golden Age of Detection, covering some of the same ground as in his excellent study Snobbery with Violence (see #61).

P. D. James writes of Dorothy L. Sayers, with side excursions on Allingham and Marsh. Julian Symons provides a useful biographical-critical summary of Dashiell Hammett, though offering little that is new. He favors the novels over the short stories and believes The Glass Key can stand comparison with any American novel of the thirties. Maurice Richardson contributes a good essay on Simenon and Patricia Highsmith. (He claims that G. D. H. and M. I. Cole anticipated the Strangers on a Train plot gimmick but does not say in what book.) Troy Kennedy Martin writes of British TV procedurals.

Editor Keating's chapter is an excellent summary of current trends in crime writing--for example, moral ambiguity, history, nostalgia, the occult, "faction." The copious illustrations cover the usual range: stills, magazine drawings, photographs of authors, and book and magazine covers.

102. La Cour, Tage, and Harald Mogensen. The Murder Book: An Illustrated History of the Detective Story. Translated from the Danish by Roy Duffell. Foreword by Julian Symons. London: Allen and Unwin, 1971. 192p. Illus. , bibl. , index. American edition, New York: Herder and Herder, 1971. 192p. Illus. , bibl. , index.

This was the first and quite possibly the best of the detective-story coffee-table books, rich in illustrations, many in color. There are tantalizing references to many European (mostly Scandinavian) mystery writers who have not been translated into English. Though they begin with Poe, the authors nod toward the Chinese detective story (and van Gulik's adaptations), William Godwin, the Newgate Calendar, and other items of prehistory in the sections following.

Though the illustrations are the main feature, the text is a worthy accomplishment. The translation is occasionally a bit stilted, and there are errors (usually a chicken-or-the-egg confusion about the origins of movie and TV novelizations), but they are relatively infrequent compared with those found in many detective-fiction reference works. Illustrations include dust jackets and book covers, movie stills, portraits of authors, magazine illustrations of stories, comic strips, cartoons, caricatures, and pulp-magazine covers.

The fine four-page multilingual bibliography of secondary sources (through 1968) turns up many items not listed elsewhere.

103. Pate, Janet. The Black Book of Villains. London: David and Charles, 1975. 120p. Illus., bibl.

Pate offers short, extensively illustrated profiles of villainous characters from literature and comics. Biographical notes, quotes from original sources, and, where appropriate, bibliographies and filmographies are included. Inclusions from mystery fiction proper are Moriarty, Godfrey Ablewhite, Mr. Hyde, Goldfinger, Fu Manchu, Carl Peterson, and Mrs. Danvers. Among the others are Captain Hook, Dracula, Lady Macbeth, Br'er Fox, Simon Legree, Uriah Heep, Bluto, and the Joker. The book has a certain exploitative inevitability about it, but there is little here for the connoisseur.

104. Pate, Janet. The Book of Sleuths. London: New English Library, 1977. 124p. Illus., bibl. American edition, Chicago: Contemporary, 1977. 124p. Illus., bibl.

In offering short biographical sketches and checklists for a group of famous fictional detectives, this volume is very similar to Otto Penzler's The Private Lives of Private Eyes ... (see #105) though generally briefer and less impressive. The entries are roughly chronological and divided into three sections: "Classical Beginnings," including eleven characters, mostly the expected (Dupin, Holmes, Lecoq, Sergeant Cuff, Father Brown, Sexton Blake, Nick Carter) but citing one obscure figure (Ralph Henderson of Charles Felix's The Notting Hill Mystery); "The Heyday," the largest section, featuring the standards (Poirot, Wimsey, Queen, Vance, Chan, Maigret) and one whimsical shocker (Rin Tin Tin) among the twenty entries; and finally "Goodbye to the

Gentlemen," including nine assorted figures (Mike Hammer, Gideon, Van der Valk, Shaft). Pate draws entries from all media, including comic-strip characters (Dick Tracy, Rip Kirby, Batman), one stage detective (J. B. Priestley's Inspector Goole), and representative movie (Inspector Clouseau) and TV (Kojak) sleuths. All the entries are illustrated, mostly with movie and TV stills.

The entries include (where appropriate) checklists of book appearances, giving both English and American first editions; film appearances; and stage and television versions. Radio is usually ignored. In the case of characters who have appeared in long series of books, Pate's bibliographic citations tend to get a little careless. In the sketch on Ellery Queen, she implies that all the EQ novels (into the sixties) were published in the United States by Stokes, a firm long out of business.

Though most of the sketches are not badly written, there are a few annoying quirks, such as an insistence on calling Charlie Chan "cuddly" (!).

105. Penzler, Otto. The Private Lives of Private Eyes, Spies, Crime Fighters, and Other Good Guys. New York: Grosset and Dunlap, 1977. viii, 214p. Illus., bibl., index.

Penzler gives the biographical treatment to 25 characters, all with literary origins although some have achieved their greatest fame through media adaptations. Beginning with the twelve greatest detectives of all time (as chosen by an Ellery Queen's Mystery Magazine poll and subsequently featured on a special series of Nicaraguan postage stamps), Penzler adds another baker's dozen. The chosen twelve are Father Brown, Chan, Dupin, Holmes, Maigret, Marlowe, Mason, Poirot, Queen, Spade, Wimsey, and Wolfe. Among the added starters are spies Modesty Blaise and James Bond, dime-novel hero Nick Carter, pulp magazine and radio crime-fighter The Shadow, and a judicious selection of private eyes.

In many cases, Penzler is covering very familiar ground. His most impressive chapters are on characters who, despite their popularity, had never received this kind of biographical treatment before: Mickey Spillane's Mike Hammer and Ernest Tidyman's Shaft. All the essays, though, are done with wit, style, and a connoisseur's knowledge of the form.

The bibliographic checklists on the various characters include first American editions, with first British only when they precede the first American. The lists are more thorough

than Pate's in The Book of Sleuths (see #104). The filmographies give main cast and director credits. Radio, television, and stage adaptations are not included. Brief biographical sketches of the characters' creators are given,
but the emphasis is on the lives of the characters. The
many and well-chosen illustrations come from the usual
sources, but portraits of the authors are notable by their
absence.

106. Quayle, Eric. The Collector's Book of Detective
Fiction. Photographs by Gabriel Monro. London: Studio
Vista, 1972. 143p. Illus., bibl., index.

　　Quayle's introduction stresses the financial soundness
of collecting detective fiction and insists it is not only a
rich person's pursuit; there are many more collectors in the
field than in years gone by. A broad definition of detective
fiction is taken in the examples cited, with the historical
discussion covering gothic novels (in the original sense), the
Newgate Calendar, Caleb Williams, and other prehistory.
There are chapters on Poe, early Victorians, Dickens, and
Collins. With the emphasis dictated by collectibility and
rarity, there is much on Fergus Hume and The Mystery of
a Hansom Cab. Much of the straight history offers little
that is original, with secondary sources leaned on heavily.
　　The illustrations, notably some beautiful color shots
of the book covers of rarities, carry the day. They are
not always coincidental with the sections in which they appear,
however. Quayle frequently cites the value of the rarities
in pounds as of the time of writing, with the equivalent amount
in dollars. The final chapter discusses ways of identifying
first editions and also warns against the more extreme forms
of bibliomania.
　　The book is most satisfying for errata buffs. Carolyn
Wells's Fleming Stone is credited with eighty cases, far too
many. Quayle thinks Phoebe Atwood Taylor wrote about Asey
Mayo under her pseudonym of Alice Tilton. S. S. Van Dine
is credited with "high speed violence and blood-letting com-
monly found in American crime novels of this and later
periods" (page 111), a statement that is comically wide of
the mark. Edmund Crispin is credited with The Glimpses
of the Moon (1972), a work long forthcoming that was not
actually published until several years later.

107. Wynn, Dilys, perpetrator. Murder Ink: The Mystery

Reader's Companion. New York: Workman, 1977. xx,
522p. Illus. , bibl. , index.

The founder of Murder Ink, the first bookstore to
deal exclusively in mysteries, pioneered in another way with
this similarly titled miscellany. It seems safe to say that
this, with the possible exception of somebody-or-other's
biography or memoirs, was the first book about mystery and
detective fiction to become a bestseller.

Early in the going, the editor urges readers not to
take the book seriously. Good advice, for this People's
Almanac for mystery buffs would either mislead, bewilder,
or infuriate any reader who took it straight as either history, criticism, or reference book. There are dozens of
articles, set up in a magazine format with numerous illustrations and sidebars. Most of the articles are original, and
the list of mystery writers, critics, and editors who have
contributed is impressive indeed--a few examples: Donald
E. Westlake, Jacques Barzun, Michael Gilbert, Isaac Asimov,
James McClure, P. D. James, and Phyllis A. Whitney.

Among the book's horrors are a list (no doubt inten-
tionally inflammatory) of the ten worst mysteries that includes The Valley of Fear and Trent's Last Case; a section
in the back giving away the solutions to some famous mysteries (bolstered by several other gratuitous giveaways that
turn up without warning throughout the book); and several
otherwise laudable bibliographies that fail to give even mini-
mally complete publishing information. These faults typify
the book's insistent frivolity. The volume could have been
accurate and responsible without sacrificing the fun that was
its main (and largely achieved) aim.

So that you won't miss the full flavor of the enterprise, I'll list a few sample offerings: a brief but meaty
article on reviewing mysteries, by Clifford A. Ridley; lists
of Nobel and Pulitzer prize winners who wrote mysteries
(without any indication of what the mysteries were); an essay
called "I. N. I. T. I. A. L. S. ," by H. R. F. Keating; a selection
of Kurt Wiese's illustrations of Walter R. Brooks's Freddy
the Pig in various disguises; a reprint of the New York
Times' Hercule Poirot obituary; an account by Ian Carmichael
of his efforts to get Lord Peter Wimsey on the BBC; a chart
by Richard R. Lingeman on how to tell Sam Spade, Philip
Marlowe, and Lew Archer apart; a critical guide by Alice
K. Turner to the various paperback series heroes (one of
the more worthwhile features, since many of these characters
have been written about seldom if ever--but, in a typical
Murder Ink lapse, their authors are not even identified!);

a history of the trench coat; an essay on false passports, by
Robin W. Winks; a mystery-oriented "Walking Tour of London,"
by Margaret Boe Birns; a selection of four Dell Mapbacks;
descriptions of American, French, and British police forces;
sections of jails and jurisprudence (American and British);
lists of mysteries with various show-biz backgrounds; an
essay (with lists, as usual incomplete) on sports mysteries,
by John L. Powers; a list of 100 items for the Sherlockian
library, by Otto Penzler (and here the information is more
complete); and various puzzles, appreciations of individual
writers, and true-crime features. That may sound like a
lot, but it's only a small fraction of what's in the book.

   Though this volume will infuriate any knowledgeable
reader more than once, it would be a mistake to get too
stuffy about its lapses and excesses. I got a great deal of
pleasure from Murder Ink, and so will any mystery buff.

108. Wynn, Dilys, perpetrator. Murderess Ink: The Better
Half of the Mystery. New York: Workman, 1979. xv,
304p. Illus. , bibl. , index.

   The sequel to Murder Ink is devoted to women and
the mystery, in the role of author, reader, detective, victim, suspect, and so forth. Like its predecessor, it is a
mild diversion, as insubstantial and unsatisfying as an issue
of People. Distinguished contributors (not all women) include Lillian O'Donnell, Patricia Moyes, Dell Shannon, Nigel
Morland, Dorothy B. Hughes, Josephine Bell, Ngaio Marsh,
Bill Pronzini, Stephen King, and Lillian de la Torre. Lightweight features include a selection of Harriet Vane paper-
dolls by Jane Langton and a shoplifter's map of Harrod's.
More substantial items include an annotated list by Kathleen
L. Maio of early mysteries by women (including a confusing
of Mary Roberts Rinehart's The Circular Staircase with her
later play The Bat that is the editor's rather than the author's
doing) and a welcome four-page article on Craig Rice, an
unjustly neglected writer.
   There are some careless errors. Rinehart's Miss
Pinkerton is said to have appeared in about twenty novels,
an outlandish overestimate. (Two is more like it.) Elizabeth Linington, who writes about Vio Varallo under the name
Lesley Egan, supposedly states in her article here (bylined
Dell Shannon) that she uses her real name of Linington for
"The Vic Vatallo books." Could the author really have made
such a double error, or is it our editor's misguided hand
again? Margaret Scherf's books are recommended to readers

who don't want humor in their mysteries--this is either a mistake or a sarcastic insult, for humor was one of their chief features.

Ultimately, <u>Murderess Ink</u> seems neither as long, as fascinating, nor as <u>angry-making</u> as its predecessor. Though insistently, incorrigibly, triumphantly lightweight, it will prove just as irresistible to the buff.   †

VII † WORKS ON INDIVIDUAL AUTHORS

ABBOT, Anthony (Fulton Oursler)

109. Oursler, Fulton. <u>Behold This Dreamer: An Autobiog-</u><u>raphy</u>. Edited and with commentary by Fulton Oursler, Jr. Boston: Little, Brown, 1964. x, 501p. Illus., index.

Oursler had many careers--editor, journalist, FBI agent, religious popularizer--so that one might expect his career as detective novelist under the name Anthony Abbot to be squeezed out of this posthumous autobiography. But there is a fair amount of reference to his mystery writing.

Surprisingly, Oursler denies that he picked Abbot as his pen name because it would come first in any alphabetical listing. This is particularly hard to believe when one considers that all the titles of the early Thatcher Colt novels began with the words <u>About the Murder of ...</u> , which seems unwieldy but alphabetically cunning. Oursler reveals that he based Police Commissioner Thatcher Colt on a combination of two men: Grover Whalen and Theodore Roosevelt. There are also references to some famous true-crime cases, including Lizzie Borden, and a section on Oursler's role in <u>The President's Mystery Story</u>, the multiauthored mystery novel based on a plot by Franklin D. Roosevelt.

Oursler had completed only a small part of his autobiography at the time of his death, and the later fragments are linked by a commentary by his son.

BENTLEY, E.C.

110. Bentley, E. C. <u>Those Days</u>. London: Constable,

1940. xv, 328p. Illus.

The title refers to the period between the 1880s and the outbreak of World War I, and Bentley perceived the book more as a portrait of that era than as an autobiography. As the book was in production, World War II was in the process of breaking out. Of principal interest for our purposes is the chapter (pages 249-261) on the writing of Trent's Last Case. Since this chapter is the source for all later recountings of the story of that landmark book, the chapter seems overfamiliar and disappointingly brief. The principal genre interest otherwise is the material on Bentley's friend G. K. Chesterton.

BIGGERS, Earl Derr

111. Chertok, Harvey, and Martha Tonge, eds. Quotations from Charlie Chan. New York: Golden, 1968. 51p. Illus.

This collection of aphorisms from Charlie Chan movies, divided into subject areas like "Of Truth," "Of Adversity," "Of Marriage," and so forth, has much to do with Hollywood and little to do with Earl Derr Biggers, whose works deserve a book-length treatment they have never received. Of most interest in this ephemeral pamphlet is a fifteen-page selection of stills from the films, giving directoral and main cast credits in the captions. The one-liners have far less appeal on the printed page than when spoken by Warner Oland or Sidney Toler.

BOUCHER, Anthony (William Anthony Parker White)

112. Boucher, Anthony, and Vincent Starrett. Sincerely, Tony; Faithfully, Vincent; The Correspondence of Anthony Boucher and Vincent Starrett. Edited by Robert W. Hahn. Chicago: Catullus, 1975. 55p. Illus. , notes.

Including 39 pages of letters and fifteen pages of explanatory notes by the editor, this small collection of exchanges between two mystery-fiction connoisseurs is both delightful, for what it contains, and frustrating, for what is missing. Many letters between the two have been lost. Among matters discussed are various Sherlockian questions, plans for Starrett's anthology of spy stories and Boucher's of great detective stories (both published by World in the

forties), and the early Edgar awards. The notes reprint
a 1939 letter by Boucher to the Saturday Review concerning
Professor Moriarty, a 1942 Boucher article about "The Man
Who Was Wanted" (the so-called 61st Sherlock Holmes story,
then unreleased and subsequently proved bogus), and Starrett's
Encyclopaedia Britannica article on "Mystery Stories."
    Published for the 1975 Chicago Bouchercon, this
pamphlet shares the characteristics of an earlier Bouchercon
volume of collected criticism (see #66): it is a delicious
but unsatisfying appetizer.

BURKE, Thomas

113. Burke, Thomas. Son of London. London: Herbert
Jenkins, n.d. (1946). 223p.

    The author of the classic short story "The Hands of
Mr. Ottermole" recalls his London youth and the British
literary and theatrical scene in the years before World War
I. The account is both beautifully written and somewhat
sketchy about dates. Not about details, though: by his feel
for the telling detail Burke makes his period come alive.

CARR, John Dickson

114. French, Larry L., ed. Notes for the Curious: A
John Dickson Carr Memorial Journal. Chesterfield, Missouri: Carrian, 1978. 32p. Bibl.

    Carr deserves a book-length biographical-critical
study, something the editor of this pamphlet intended to
provide eventually--before his untimely death in an automobile
accident. This is a well-intended but somewhat disorganized
and tentative grab bag of tributes, quotation, bibliography,
and a chronology of Carr's life. Major contributors include
Robert E. Briney, Richard Sneary, and editor French.

CASPARY, Vera

115. Caspary, Vera. The Secrets of Grown-ups. New
York: McGraw-Hill, 1979. 287p. Illus., index.

    The author of Laura offers a beautifully written and
apparently very honest and unsparing autobiography. How-

ever, it is mostly personal and reveals relatively little about her writings. The only mystery-related figures to appear as characters are Fulton Oursler (a less-than-favorable portrait) and the team of Gwen Bristow and Bruce Manning.

CHANDLER, Raymond

116. Bruccoli, Matthew J. Raymond Chandler: A Checklist (The Serif Series: Bibliographies and Checklists). Kent, Ohio: Kent State University Press, 1968. ix, 35p.

Bruccoli's first effort in book form at a Chandler bibliography is a fine one, though now superseded by the descriptive bibliography of eleven years later (see #117). Included are Chandler's books in all editions, plus first book and periodical appearances of stories, articles, reviews, newspaper columns, letters, poems, blurbs, and interviews.

117. Bruccoli, Matthew J. Raymond Chandler: A Descriptive Bibliography (Pittsburgh Series in Bibliography). Pittsburgh: University of Pittsburgh Press, 1979. xv, 146p. Illus., index.

This impressive production gives full details (down to the binding and typography) of all first editions of all of Chandler's books and reproduces title pages, dust jackets, and paperback covers. All known later editions are also listed and numbered. Following the main section are listings of reprint collections and omnibuses, contributions to books, magazine and newspaper appearances, and motion-picture work. There is a short list of major works about Chandler. This is obviously an essential volume for the serious Chandler collector.

118. Chandler, Raymond. Raymond Chandler Speaking. Edited by Dorothy Gardiner and Kathrine Sorley Walker. London: Hamish Hamilton, 1962. Illus., index. American edition, Boston: Houghton Mifflin, 1962. 271p. Illus., index.

This selection of Chandler's letters (with a few articles interspersed) is arranged topically, bringing together the author's thoughts on himself, the mystery novel, the craft of writing, the film world and TV, publishing, cats, famous crimes, and his novels, short stories, and Philip Marlowe. Also included are a previously unpublished short story, "A Couple of Writers," and the opening chapters of an unfinished novel about Marlowe, The Poodle Springs Story.

Not all great writers are great letter-writers, but Chandler undeniably was. His ruminations on the death of his wife are poetic and moving. His acerbic comments on the works of other mystery writers are (agree or not) acutely reasoned and economically expressed. His appreciations of such writers as Erle Stanley Gardner, R. Austin Freeman, and Elizabeth Sanxay Holding are equally pointed and interesting. (If Chandler had ever done any mystery reviewing on a regular basis, he might have been the greatest critic the field has ever seen.) On Hollywood and the publishing world, he is lethally witty. Of all the works listed in this bibliography, this is probably one of the two or three best.

119.   Chandler, Raymond, and James M. Fox. Letters. Edited by James Pepper. Santa Barbara, California: Neville + Yellin, 1978.   viii, 66p.

In letters dating from December 20, 1950, to January 7, 1956, the two writers exchange opinions and information both professional and personal. Although Chandler was a great letter-writer, and Fox isn't bad either, this is basically an ephemeral item, including even such antiquarian information as the directions to Chandler's house in La Jolla. Both Ross Macdonald and Alfred Hitchcock receive slighting references from Chandler, and in a discussion of Casino Royale he seems less a Fleming fan than has been suggested elsewhere. In his first letter to Fox, Chandler suggests that he explore the comparatively fresh ground of espionage in preference to the overworked hardboiled private-eye field. Fox took the advice.

120.   Durham, Philip. Down These Mean Streets a Man Must Go: Raymond Chandler's Knight. Chapel Hill: University of North Carolina Press, 1963.   viii, 173p.   Bibl., index.

A pioneering work on Chandler, this may well be the first full-length critical study of any author known primarily for mystery fiction. It is a totally readable book, something that (sadly and oddly enough) many critical studies by professors of English are anything but. Chapter four, "The City," about Chandler's depiction of Los Angeles and how it changed over the years, is one of the very few nonfiction articles ever to appear in Ellery Queen's Mystery Magazine. Another advantage Durham has over some other academics who invade the mystery field is that he seems to have a considerable knowledge of detective fiction aside from that of his subject.

With all the writing that has been done on Chandler since, this remains a valuable summary. An analysis of Chandler's "cannibalization" of his pulp stories for his novels is especially interesting.

121. Gross, Miriam, ed. The World of Raymond Chandler. Introduction by Patricia Highsmith. London: Weidenfeld and Nicolson, 1977. ix, 190p. Illus., bibl. American edition, New York: A & W, 1977. ix, 190p. Illus., bibl.

Here is a splendid collection of essays, mostly by British writers and critics, illuminating aspects of Chandler's life and works. It is a worthy companion to Frank McShane's biography (see #122), to which many of the writers refer. Among the contributors are Julian Symons, on the pulp stories; Billy Wilder, interviewed about his experiences collaborating with Chandler on the screenplay for Double Indemnity; John Houseman, about Chandler's work on The Blue Dahlia; Philip French, about the various actors to play Marlowe; Dilys Powell, about Chandler's relations with his much older wife, Cissy; Michael Gilbert, his reminiscences as Chandler's British lawyer; and Frank Norman, a beautifully written reminiscence by a Chandler protégé.

122. McShane, Frank. The Life of Raymond Chandler. New York: Dutton, 1976. xii, 306p. Illus., bibl., index.

The first full-scale biography of Chandler is an excellent piece of work, well written and balancing the biographical and critical elements perfectly. The section of photographs includes many unfamiliar ones. Readers well versed in mystery fiction, though, will find the volume error-prone when it goes beyond Chandler into the field at large. McShane knows his subject and his work well but, by his own admission, is not interested in or well informed about crime fiction generally. Thus, he gets names wrong ("Lewis" Nebel, Geoffrey "Holmes") and accepts without challenge Chandler's own statements, such as one casting the incomparable mystery critic Anthony Boucher as a self-serving villain, mainly (it seems) on the basis of his dislike of The Little Sister. Boucher wrote favorably of Chandler's other books and was certainly not the short-sighted advocate of one kind of mystery that Chandler suggests.

123. Pendo, Stephen. Raymond Chandler on Screen: His Novels into Film. Metuchen, New Jersey: Scarecrow, 1976. xv, 240p. Illus., bibl., index.

Pendo discusses in exhaustive detail seven films based on six of Chandler's novels: Murder, My Sweet (based on Farewell, My Lovely), The Big Sleep (Bogart version), Lady in the Lake, The Brasher Doubloon (based on The High Window), Marlowe (based on The Little Sister), and Farewell, My Lovely. Since the main concern is with the character of Marlowe, the adaptations of the novels as vehicles for other sleuths are not discussed. Book and film plots are compared in parallel columns, sometimes with a third column for the film's script. There is much information here, including full credits of the films and some very well-produced stills. There may be too much depth here for the casual reader, but the student of Marlowe (on the page or on the screen) will find Pendo's book valuable.

CHARTERIS, Leslie (Leslie Charles Bowyer Yin)

124. Alexandersson, Jan, and Iwan Hedman. Leslie Charteris och Helgonet under 5 Decennier en Bio-bibliografi. Strängnäs, Sweden: DAST-Förlag, 1973. 124p. Illus., index.

Although the text of this bibliography is in Swedish, it has several features that make it valuable to the English-language reader: a complete descriptive bibliography of Charteris's books in first edition through 1972, a list of films based on Charteris's works, and a list of Saint TV episodes.

125. Lofts, W. O. G., and Derek Adley. The Saint and Leslie Charteris. London: Howard Baker, 1970. 134p. Bibl. American edition, Bowling Green, Ohio: Bowling Green University Popular Press, 1972. 134p. Bibl.

The first book about Charteris proves a disappointment.

The biographical half is vague, uncritical, and sketchy, and
the bibliographic half includes only British editions, which
is perfectly acceptable in the British version but seems odd
in the American reprint. The bibliography, identifying original magazine appearances of the tales, seems otherwise
thorough and well done.

CHEYNEY, Peter (Reginald Southouse Cheyney)

126. Harrison, Michael. Peter Cheyney: Prince of Hokum.
London: Neville Spearman, 1954. vii, 303p. Illus.

The readable, chatty biography of Lemmy Caution's
creator is marked by a tendency to get off on entertaining
tangents, a characteristic of Harrison's more recent works
on Jack the Ripper and Sherlock Holmes. The work seems
a trifle padded--including as it does more family background,
music-hall and theatrical history, and detail on the tracing
of Cheyney's school records than seems strictly necessary--
but the always-lively Harrison manufactures better padding
than most.
    Cheyney emerges as a pretty unattractive character.
His political, social, and racial views are rather glossed
over, but one gets the idea. In the closing pages, Harrison
finally gets around to discussing, and quoting at length, the
contents of Cheyney's novels and pretty well discourages the
reader (this one, anyway) from looking them up.

CHRISTIE, Agatha

127. Barnard, Robert. A Talent to Deceive: An Appreciation of Agatha Christie. London: Collins, 1980. 203p.
Bibl. American edition, New York: Dodd, Mead, 1980. x,
213p. Bibl.

This is the first book-length critical study of Agatha
Christie and, by a considerable margin, the best book to
date about the creator of Hercule Poirot and Miss Marple.
In 87 pages of appendix, the author presents a bibliography
and short-story index, compiled by Louise Barnard; a bibliography of secondary sources; a critically annotated list, arranged alphabeticaly, of all of Christie's books; and a list,
with main credits, of Christie films.
    The analyses are quite frank, and it is to the credit
of the publishers that they would bring out a book so openly

critical of many of their bestselling author's novels, especially the later ones.

In the 126-page main text, Barnard considers all the
major criticisms of Christie as a writer: rudimentary characterization, insipid style, vague settings, reactionary social
and racial viewpoints. He gives them all full play, finally
concluding that they are ultimately more or less beside the
point. The book proves Christie's work can stand up to a
really searching analysis and survive. Though this is not a
biography, Barnard does devote part of a chapter to Christie's
mysterious disappearance in 1926, but only insofar as he
believes the experience affected her later work. Barnard
closely examines three Christies as supreme examples of
her art, choices that may surprise some fans: Hercule
Poirot's Christmas, Five Little Pigs (Murder in Retrospect),
and A Murder Is Announced. He notes that the solution to
Crooked House was anticipated by Margery Allingham in The
White Cottage Mystery but is apparently unaware of the definitive use of the gimmick in Barnaby Ross's The Tragedy
of Y.

128. Behre, Frank. Studies in Agatha Christie's Writings:
The Behavior of a GOOD (GREAT) DEAL, A LOT, LOTS,
MUCH, PLENTY, MANY, A GOOD (GREAT) MANY (Gothen-
berg Studies in English, No. 19). Stockholm: Almqvist and
Wiksell, 1967. 203p. Bibl.

Though the preface and some of the commentary make
clear the author's fondness for Agatha Christie's writings,
this highly technical linguistic study of her work offers virtually nothing for the nonspecialist reader or student of detective fiction.

129. Christie, Agatha. An Autobiography. London: Collins, 1977. 542p. Illus., index. American edition, New
York: Dodd, Mead, 1977. xiii, 529p. Illus., index.

Agatha Christie's own account of her life has a good
deal of charm and wisdom, as well as insights into her
creative processes. It fails as an autobiography, however,
because of its reticence. The disappearance in 1926, which
was one of the central events in Christie's life, is not even
referred to, while nostalgic childhood memories of less relevance are detailed at length. It was, of course, her privi-
lege to write the kind of autobiography she wanted to, and

there is much here that is entertaining and enlightening.
While some devoted readers will be willing to search for it,
most will probably gain more enjoyment from any of her
novels.

130. East, Andy. Andy East's Agatha Christie Quizbook.
New York: Drake, 1975. 169p.

     This is just what it sounds like: a bunch of quizzes
about the works of Agatha Christie followed by the answers.
This may be the only such work devoted to the works of a
single mystery writer, save, of course, Conan Doyle. It is
fun but has little if any value to the student or scholar.

131. Feinman, Jeffrey. The Mysterious World of Agatha
Christie. New York: Award, 1975. 190p. Illus., bibl.

     Though this biography-appreciation begins well, with
the account of a doctor's use of Christie's The Pale Horse
to crack a real-life poisoning case, its gee-whiz style and
ragged organization make it the worst book about Christie,
surpassing even Ramsey (see #134). Feinman brings in
everything but the kitchen sink (Detection Club oath, Poirot
obituary, Mousetrap party, Edmund Wilson) to fill the pages,
and the chapters are often repetitious and contradictory
enough to be by different authors--if the pedestrian style
were not so constant. The squibs on the various novels in
an annotated list (and an incomplete one to boot) are unmatched
in their puerility. Never were Christie's endings given away
more uselessly.

132. Keating, H. R. F., ed. Agatha Christie: First Lady
of Crime. London: Weidenfeld and Nicolson, 1977. 224p.
Illus., bibl., index. American edition, New York: Holt,
Rinehart, and Winston, 1977. 224p. Illus., bibl., index.

     This splendid collection of essays, most of them the
work of her fellow crime novelists, examine every aspect of
the Christie oeuvre. Repetition is minimal, and the multiauthored collection achieves a cohesive whole that is a tribute
to Keating's editing. Among the contributors are Julian
Symons, Edmund Crispin, Michael Gilbert, Colin Watson,
and Christianna Brand. Though most of the contributors
manage to keep the endings (even of Roger Ackroyd) a secret,

be warned that the article by Emma Lathen is booby-trapped
with solution giveaways, as well as doubtful statements (for
example, that sports attendance is plummeting in the United
States). Keating's final article makes a rather startling
suggestion about Hercule Poirot. J. C. Trewin surveys
Christie's theatrical work, and Philip Jenkinson discusses
the films, giving surprising approval to the generally despised
Tony Randall-as-Poirot film, The Alphabet Murders. Illustrations are plentiful.

133. Murdoch, Derrick. The Agatha Christie Mystery.
Toronto: Pagurian, 1976. 192p. Illus., bibl., index.

In one of the better books about Christie, Murdoch
combines biography and criticism--though appreciation might
be a more accurate word. Though he does not perform the
book-by-book analysis later to come from Robert Barnard
(see #127), he does approach the evaluative more than most
other early books about Christie. Perhaps from a lack of
material to flesh out the book, he brings in more general
detective-fiction history than would seem necessary. Following the main text comes a poem, "Elegy for Agatha Christie,"
by Pamela Stewart; chronological checklists of the books and
films (with principal credits); and a history of the plays in
chart form. There is a useful secondary-source bibliography.

134. Ramsey, G. C. Agatha Christie: Mistress of Mystery.
New York: Dodd, Mead, 1967. 124p. Illus., bibl.

The pioneering volume on Christie, this includes a
short biography/appreciation with several appendixes listing
her works since 1967, including brief plot descriptions on
the novels. The final sections give words and music of
nursery rhymes used in Christie stories. Completely superseded by later and better books on Christie, Ramsey's volume
is most memorable today for a rather vicious (and in my
opinion wholly unwarranted) attack on Elizabeth Linington's
homage to Christie in the novel Greenmask (though neither
Linington nor her book are referred to by name).

135. Riley, Dick, and Pam McAllister, eds. The Bedside,
Bathtub, and Armchair Companion to Agatha Christie. Introduction by Julian Symons. New York: Ungar, 1979. xix,
330p. Illus., bibl., index.

This is the Christie coffee-table book, very much along the lines of Murder Ink and Murderess Ink (see #107 and 108)--large-formated, generously illustrated, but far less than meets the eye. The main feature is lengthy plot summaries of all the novels, stopping short of giving away the solutions. To which are the good ones, though, the reader gets not a clue, except in the quotes from Christie's Autobiography (see #129) that precede most entries. Other features include a fan letter from Lillian Carter, an article on English tea, Christie crossword puzzles, an annotated filmography (brief credits and as uncritical as the plot summaries), recipes for favorite English dishes, an article on poisons, interviews with fans, and a profile of Margaret Rutherford. You get the idea.

136. Robyns, Gwen. The Mystery of Agatha Christie. Garden City, New York: Doubleday, 1978. xiii, 247p. Illus. , bibl. , index.

This is the biography of choice, surprisingly for a number of reasons. The author is a specialist in show-biz bios (Grace Kelley, Vivien Leigh) and claims no particular interest or expertise in detective fiction. And she had no official cooperation from Christie's family, relying on the Autobiography (see #129), interviews, and press accounts of an earlier day for her material. Not surprisingly, there is no critical content here to speak of, but the book offers more information about Christie's life than any source except the Autobiography, while getting into areas Christie shunned in her own account.

In a rare slip-up, Robyns refers to mystery writer Nigel "Moorland," who for some reason seems especially prone to having his name misspelled (see #90).

Robyns won the Mystery Writers of America Edgar award for 1978 in the biographical-critical category.

137. Wynne, Nancy Blue. An Agatha Christie Chronology. New York: Ace, 1976. 266p. Bibl.

One of the first book-length sources about Christie, this volume has value as a bibliography and collection of plot summaries, briefer than those in The Bedside, Bathtub ... Book (see #135). The disappointingly slight evaluative content belongs to the if-you-can't-say-something-nice-say-nothing-at-all school of literary criticism. It is interesting

that Wynne believes The Mystery of the Blue Train, despised
by Christie, to be among her best books. Be warned that
Wynne sometimes reveals solutions, and the depth of her
analysis is never sufficient to justify it.

COLLINS, Wilkie

138. Andrew, R. V. Wilkie Collins: A Critical Survey of
His Prose Fiction with a Bibliography (The Fiction of Popular
Culture). New York: Garland, 1979. 358p.

This photographic reprint of a 1959 doctoral thesis,
presented to Potchefstroom University for C. H. E. , South
Africa, may have been worth publishing as a book. It is
an exhaustive if not a lively survey of Collins's writings,
perhaps in need of a little tightening. The typing job could
have been better--it is rather depressing to see twenty-year-
old strikeovers preserved for posterity between hard covers
(and for $35 at that!).
In a bit of critical originality, Andrew advances The
Law and the Lady, not The Moonstone, as Collins's première
contribution to detective fiction. As in Murch (see #2), the
style of underlining the titles of both novels and short stories
in confusing and irritating.

139. Ashley, Robert. Wilkie Collins. London: Arthur
Barker, 1952. 144p. Bibl. , index. American edition, New
York: Roy, 1952. 144p. Bibl. , index.

In a good, brief biography with a critical emphasis,
Ashley claims The Law and the Lady is much closer to
modern detective fiction than The Moonstone, though he does
not carry his approval of it as far as Andrew (see #138).
He also identifies I Say No and My Lady's Money as having
been unfairly neglected by detective-story historians. In
the latter, Old Sharon, the eccentric detective, says, "Suspect the very last person on which suspicion could possibly
fall. " Unfortunately, Sharon does not detect much in the
novel. Like Kenneth Robinson (see #143), Ashley challenges
the claim that Collins declined in popularity late in his career.

140. Beetz, Kirk H. Wilkie Collins: An Annotated Bibliography, 1889-1976 (The Scarecrow Author Bibliographies, No.
35). Metuchen, New Jersey: Scarecrow, 1978. viii, 167p.
Index.

Following a 21-page chronology of Collins's life and works (with its own index), Beetz presents a 688-item bibliography of books, periodical articles, and dissertations. The listing is divided into three sections: editions of Collins's works, critical and scholarly works about him, and selected book reviews. Many of the entries, especially in the critical section, have useful and lengthy annotations. Reviews of the book-length Collins studies are cited. Many widely varying books with some Collins content are included. This is a useful, far-reaching, and thorough work of bibliographic scholarship, recommended for more thorough coverage of the books about Collins than can be presented here. Beetz includes an index to authors, editors, and illustrators, and a subject index.

141. Davis, Nuel Pharr. The Life of Wilkie Collins. Introduction by Gordon N. Ray. Urbana: University of Illinois Press, 1956. 360p. Illus. , bibl. , index.

Other commentators on Collins have flayed Davis for failing to label as conjecture the inferences he draws about Collins's life, mostly regarding his relationship with his father, from the supposedly autobiographical content of his fiction. Be that as it may, this biography is both well written and meticulously documented, even if others may draw differing conclusions from the documentation. There are many details here of the financial aspects of Collins's career.

142. Marshall, William H. Wilkie Collins (Twayne's English Authors Series, Vol. 94). New York: Twayne, 1970. 159p. Bibl. , index.

Claiming to be the first full-length study solely concerned with Collins's work rather than his life, Marshall's book follows the familiar Twayne pattern, including a biographical chronology, a title-by-title treatment of Collins's works, a summation of his achievement, a section of notes and references, and an excellent bibliography of primary and secondary sources. Marshall continues to regard The Moonstone as the first English detective novel, an old tag pretty well discredited in the absence of a qualifying adjective.

143. Page, Norman, ed. Wilkie Collins: The Critical Heritage (The Critical Heritage Series). London: Routledge and Kegan Paul, 1974. xvi, 288p. Bibl. , index.

In the familiar format of a very useful series, Page has gathered contemporary reviews of Collins's books. Some letters are also quoted. Of the 86 items included, fifteen cover The Woman in White (by far the largest section) and seven concern The Moonstone. Henry James is notable among the reviewers (mostly anonymous) quoted, while other notables include letter-writers Dickens, Edward Fitzgerald, and George Meredith; parodist Bret Harte; and memoirist Anthony Trollope. The collection not only sheds light on Collins's work but also reflects developments and changes in book reviewing from the 1850s to the late 1880s, a period longer than that covered by any of Collins's notable contemporaries. An introduction summarizes Collins's literary career and critical reception in 36 pages. A bibliography of more recent secondary sources is included.

The continuing theme is that Collins was far more successful with readers than critics, though it is not true that in the novels of his last years he fell into disfavor and obscurity. The novels through Poor Miss Finch (1872) have several reviews each, while the later novels are dealt with much more briefly. The final nine entries are general considerations, most written on the occasion of Collins's death. A. C. Swinburne and Andrew Lang are notable among the overall critics.

144. Robinson, Kenneth. Wilkie Collins: A Biography. New York: Macmillan, 1952. 348p. Illus. , bibl. , index.

This is a sound and readable critical biography, enlivened by quotations from Collins's amusing letters, especially inspired when asking for money. (Unfortunately, many other Collins letters, including those he wrote to his friend Dickens, were destroyed.) In the section on The Woman in White, Robinson offers much firsthand material about Collins's working methods. There is also an interesting account of the stage version of The Moonstone and how it differed from the novel. There is much material on Collins's involvement with Dickens in amateur theatricals. Robinson ultimately blames Collins's decline as a writer on his opium addiction.

145. Sayers, Dorothy L. Wilkie Collins: A Critical and Biographical Study. Edited by E. R. Gregory. Toledo, Ohio: Friends of the University of Toledo Libraries, 1977. 120p. Illus.

For the last quarter-century of her life, Sayers was rumored to be working on a definitive study of Collins. The five chapters she actually completed, bringing her subject's life up to 1855, five years before The Woman in White and thirteen before The Moonstone, are published here for the first time with informative introduction and notes by Gregory. This well-written fragment suggests that the finished book would have been a major contribution to detective-story scholarship.

CREASEY, John

146. John Creasey in Print 1970. London: Hodder and Stoughton, 1969. 73p. Illus., bibl.

Obviously, this promotional publication makes no pretense of offering a critical evaluation of John Creasey's works, though it does quote numerous favorable reviews. It has considerable bibliographic value, though, differentiating among all of Creasey's pseudonyms and listing the entries, with British in-print data as of 1970. Introductions to each section summarize the series' backgrounds and discuss the differences in style among the pseudonyms. Astonishingly, even the long lists of books contained in this pamphlet do not cover Creasey's whole output--the Mark Kilby books, as by Robert Caine Frazer, are not included.

DAVIS, Frederick C.

147. Carr, Nick. America's Secret Service Ace (Pulp Classics, No. 7). Oak Lawn, Illinois: Robert Weinberg, 1974. 64p. Illus., bibl.

This overwhelmingly exhaustive fan study discusses the pulp hero Operator 5, whose adventures appeared between 1934 and 1939 in a magazine of the same name. The stories were signed by Curtis Steele, a house name that covered first Frederick C. Davis, later Emile C. Tepperman, and possibly other writers as well. Davis, who later did many Crime Club detective novels under his own name and as Stephen Ransome, apparently created the characters and did most of the Operator 5 novels. Unfortunately, this book tells little of Davis, and its combination of overdone detail and awkward writing style renders it worthwhile only to the most fanatical pulp-hero buffs.

DIXON, Franklin W. (Leslie W. McFarlane, and others)

148. McFarlane, Leslie W. Ghost of the Hardy Boys: An Autobiography. Toronto: Methuen/Two Continents, 1976. 211p.

The Canadian author of many of the Hardy Boys juvenile detective novels (under the famed house name of Franklin W. Dixon) offers his entertaining and humorous autobiography. Recounting his experiences as a pen-for-hire of the Stratemeyer syndicate, McFarlane states that he tried to make the Hardy Boys books better than his earlier work, mainly by adding a touch of humor and descriptions of food whenever possible. He also describes his disillusionment at picking up current editions of the Hardy books and finding them rewritten, updated, and sanitized into wholesome blandness. It might have been preferable, though, for the memoir to include even more about the Hardys and the operation of the Stratemeyer syndicate and less of the author's digressions, such as a chapter on Horatio Alger, interesting but nothing new.

DONOVAN, Dick (J. E. Preston Muddock)

149. "Donovan, Dick" [J. E. Preston Muddock]. Pages from an Adventurous Life. London: Werner Laurie, n.d. (1907). xvi, 352p. Illus., index.

Muddock was in India at the time of the mutiny, saw the last woman hanged in Britain, had "a real good time and plenty of fun" in America during the Civil War, knew a lot of famous actors (including Henry Irving and Joseph Jefferson), reported on the Charles Bravo murder case, and knew Artemas Ward. This is a typical Victorian autobiography, full of anecdotes, famous people known, and obituaries of friends. Self-analysis is notably absent.

Muddock's life seemingly revolved around a London literary society called the Savage Club, and he spends much space thumbnail-sketching his fellow members, most unfamiliar names but among them Arthur Morrison, "still little more than a youth," whose "books, including some very clever detective stories, will be known to generations yet unborn."

Surely, Morrison's works have outlived the stories Muddock wrote as Dick Donovan. Though the Donovan name is used to sell the book, not until page 332 does he get around to discussing his detective fiction, largely disdaining it and insisting he did it only for the money. Stuffy and condescending as his attitude toward such fiction is, he dutifully trots out the obligatory Celebrated Reader (in this case, Prince Bismarck). Any reference to his famous contemporaries in the game, Conan Doyle and Sherlock Holmes, is oddly lacking.

DU MAURIER, Daphne

150. du Maurier, Daphne. Growing Pains: The Shaping of a Writer. London: Gollancz, 1977. 173p. Illus. American edition under title Myself When Young: The Shaping of a Writer. Garden City, New York: Doubleday, 1977. 204p. Illus., index.

The author covers her life from age three to 25 and the publication of her first novel. Although there is little in the book about mystery writing per se, the account has the charm of the author's other writings, and there are occasional foreshadowings of books (like Rebecca) to come. From the age of twelve, du Maurier quotes occasionally from diaries she kept at the time. Among the unexpected characters is Basil Rathbone, on whom the youthful Daphne had a crush. Edgar Wallace, in many of whose plays Daphne's father, Gerald, appeared, is frequently mentioned but never stays on stage for long.

FAIRLIE, Gerard

151. Fairlie, Gerard. With Prejudice: Almost an Autobiography. London: Hodder and Stoughton, 1952. 255p. Index.

Fairlie, a thriller writer far better known in Great Britain than the United States, was the original model for Bulldog Drummond, created by his friend Sapper (H. C. McNeile). Fairlie continued the Drummond series after McNeile's death. Though he has some of the insular opinions and attitudes one might expect of Drummond's model, Fairlie comes across as a sincere, likable fellow in this memoir. His anecdotes about Sapper are the most notable feature of the book, his rather ingenuous and obvious remarks about Hollywood and the film business the least.

FLEMING, Ian

152. Amis, Kingsley. The James Bond Dossier. London: Jonathan Cape, 1965. 159p. Bibl. American edition, New York: New American Library, 1965. 147p. Bibl.

The distinguished English novelist, who himself added to the Bond series, with Colonel Sun (as by Robert Markham), here examines the saga and defends Fleming against his critics. He contrasts the supposedly ruthless Bond with more genuinely violent characters like Mike Hammer and Bulldog Drummond. He goes through the obligatory discussions of Bond's women and adversaries, his brand-name dropping and morality, with a good deal more style and wit than most other commentators. In his conclusion, he makes clear his extreme admiration of Fleming by ranking him with Jules Verne, Rider Haggard, and Conan Doyle. In appendixes, he discusses Fleming's links with science fiction and acquits the author of sadism (because enjoyment is lacking). A reference guide charts the main features of all the Bond stories through The Man with the Golden Gun (with columns for places, girl, villain, Bond's friends, highspots, and remarks).
This is decidedly one of the best books on Fleming.

153. Bond, Mary Wickham. How 007 Got His Name. London: Collins, 1966. 62p. Illus.

The wife of the ornithologist who wrote Birds of the West Indies, and whose solid, simple name Ian Fleming borrowed for 007, tells us something about her husband, their meeting with Fleming, and how the Bond phenomenon affected their lives. This essay may have the slightest excuse to be a book of any of the exploitative outpouring of let's-cash-in-on-Bond ventures in the mid-sixties. The wit and charm of the writing disarm criticism somewhat, though. When they discovered Fleming had borrowed the name James Bond for his hero, Mrs. Bond writes, "I went ahead and read all the Double-O-Seven books published to date, my husband having got the idea in Dr. No and let it go at that" (page 17).

154. Boyd, Ann. The Devil with James Bond. Richmond, Virginia: John Knox, 1967. 123p.

Apparently inspired by Robert L. Short's theological
study of Peanuts (published by the same firm), Boyd's study
depicts the Bond saga as a retelling of the St. George legend.
Fleming's intent was "to name and destroy the modern gods
of our society which are actually the expressions of the de-
monic in contemporary disguises" (page 35). Valid or not,
Boyd's premise is entertainingly argued in a chatty style
much given to puns. Fleming is compared to such figures
as Chaucer, Langland, Bunyan, and Spencer, and his hero
is ultimately compared to German theologian Dietrich Bon-
hoeffer. The book is somewhere on the borderline between
real literary criticism and the use of a popular subject to
make theological points. (In the last ten pages, Bond and
Fleming are not even mentioned!)

155. Bryce, Ivar. You Only Live Once: Memories of Ian
Fleming. London: Weidenfeld and Nicolson, 1975. 142p. Illus.,
bibl.

Years after the major outpouring of books about Fleming came this reminiscence of a friend, capped by a list of
Fleming's books and the inscriptions he wrote in copies given
to Bryce. Belonging to that genre of books owing their
existence to acquaintance with someone famous (John F.
Kennedy or Marilyn Monroe or John Wayne), this is a plea-
sant but relatively ephemeral item for completist Fleming
collections. Bryce was codefendant with Fleming in the
litigation over the novel Thunderball and its film treatment
origin.

156. del Buono, Oreste, and Umberto Eco, eds. The Bond
Affair. Translated from the Italian by R. A. Downie. London: Macdonald, 1966. 173p. Bibl.

This is an odd item, probably the only book on thriller
and detective fiction to be translated into English from Italian,
a language not noted for its contributions to the genre. There
are eight essays. The lead article by Lietta Tornabuoni
describes the Bond phenomenon in general; while much of
the material is familiar, the emphasis on 007's impact in
Italy makes it of interest. Tornabuoni also sketches the
personality and background of James Bond. In the longest
essay, coeditor Eco discusses Fleming's narrative method in
considerable detail, likening a Bond novel to a Harlem Globe-

trotters basketball game. (Eco's rather bowdlerized explanation to his Italian readers of the name Pussy Galore is amusing.) Others include Romano Calisi on Bond as myth (turgid, pretentious, and heavily italicized), Furio Colombo with the obligatory essay on Bond's women (one of the better such), Fausto Antonini psychoanalyzing Bond's readership, G. B. Zorzoli on the technology of the Bond novels, Andrea Barbato on the relationship of the Bond films to real-life political events, and Laura Lilli with a very useful summary of the critical response to James Bond.

These essays represent serious analysis, not, like some of the English-language works on Fleming, quicky attempts to cash in on a fad.

157. Gant, Richard. Ian Fleming: The Man with the Golden Pen. London: Mayflower-Dell, 1966. 172p.

One of the glut of Fleming biographies to appear in the mid-sixties, this one is a brief, totally nonscholarly job (without notes or bibliography), though not badly written or overly exploitative. The facts and quotes are mostly familiar from other secondary sources, earlier or contemporaneous, though only Amis (see #152) among the other commentators is referred to specifically.

158. Lane, Sheldon, ed. For Bond Lovers Only. London: Panther, 1965. 172p. Illus. American edition, New York: Dell, 1965. 156p. Illus.

Apart from a nice pin-up gallery of Bond's cinematic girlfriends, this collection of journalistic interviews and appreciations is pretty thin stuff. Sean Connery is interviewed at a time when he was apparently somewhat happier about playing Bond than he later became. A meeting between Fleming and Len Deighton is described, as is another between Fleming and Simenon, one of the more interesting pieces with much about the attitudes and working methods of both writers. A very short interview with Raymond Chandler about Bond is less fruitful. The final piece is a reminiscence of Fleming by Allen Dulles.

159. Pearson, John. The Life of Ian Fleming. London: Jonathan Cape, 1966. 352p. Illus., index. American edition, New York: McGraw-Hill, 1966. vii, 338p. Illus., index.

This is the standard life, offering more detail about Fleming's various careers than any other source. Fleming emerges as a man of great promise and ability who never really found his niche until he created James Bond, tossing off Casino Royale in an apparently effortless eight weeks just as something to do in preference to watching his wife paint. In addition to the biographical details, Pearson offers some worthy critical analysis and speculation about the origins of some of the events and characters in Fleming's books. He observes, for example, that as a child Fleming frequently called his formidable mother, M....

The best thing to be said of this book is that Fleming really does emerge as a personality, including (though Pearson admires Fleming) his less admirable traits of moodiness, snobbishness, and self-promotion. Fleming's sense of humor, an element that (according to Pearson) was totally lacking in the James Bond novels, comes over strongly in this book.

160. Richler, Mordecai. Notes on an Endangered Species and Others. New York: Knopf, 1974. 212p.

Only the first essay (pages 3-35) in this collection deals with Fleming and Bond, but it seems worth noting here for its exposure of the veiled anti-Semitism Richler finds running through the 007 novels. He finds it more muted but just as pernicious as that found in the works of John Buchan, Sapper, and William Le Queux. This is among the most frankly unfriendly pieces of Bond criticism to find its way between covers and (as would be expected from its author) among the best written. Richler disputes Kingsley Amis's statement (see #152) that appreciation for an author is the sine qua non for writing about him at length. Writes Richler, "It is equally valid to examine an author's work in detail if you find his books morally repugnant and the writer himself an insufferably self-satisfied boor" (page 35).

161. Snelling, O. F. Double O Seven, James Bond: A Report. London: Neville Spearman/Holland Press, 1964. 160p. American edition, New York: New American Library, 1965. 127p.

Inspired by Richard Usborne's Clubland Heroes (see #60) and its account of Yates, Buchan, and Sapper, Snelling produced the first of the sixties' flood of studies of Fleming and Bond. Written while Fleming was still alive and working, the book covers novels only through On Her Majesty's Secret Service. The emphasis is strictly on Bond's adventures, not Fleming's biography. The five chapters cover his predecessors, his image, his women (the longest section), his adversaries, and his future. Aside from its primacy in the field, the book is quite entertaining and readable.

162. Starkey, Lycurgus M. , Jr. James Bond's World of Values. Nashville, Tennessee: Abingdon, 1966. 96p.

Unlike Ann Boyd's version (see #154), this theological view of the Bond phenomenon is unfriendly toward Fleming and his creation. According to Starkey, Bond's values challenge the Christian faith and ethic in five areas: "sex, sadism, status, leisure time, and a narrow nationalism" (page 11). Here, there is absolutely no pretense of literary criticism (nor, it should be added, any call for censorship) but rather a series of Christian moral lessons spun off from a Bondian starting point. The perspective is not fundamentalist but liberal, both politically and theologically.

163. Tanner, William. The Book of Bond; or Every Man His Own 007. London: Jonathan Cape, 1965. 111p. Illus. American edition, New York: Viking, 1965. 111p. Illus.

In a novelty item taking the form of a tongue-in-cheek self-help book, the reader desiring to emulate Bond is advised in such areas as food, drink, exercise, clothes, cars, smokes, gambling, and girls, with references to the Bond novels where the various commodities are referred to. It's a very ephemeral fad item, for completist collections only.

164. Zieger, Henry A. Ian Fleming: The Spy Who Came in with the Gold. New York: Duell, Sloan, and Pearce, 1965. 150p.

Though reasonably well written, the biographical part of this quicky is very much a scissors-and-paste job. The fictional dialogue in the opening warns the reader not to expect much. Some of the critical comments in Zeiger's final chapter, including a contention that the Bond novels in fact lack suspense, are more interesting.

FOX, James M. (see CHANDLER, Raymond, #119)

FRANCES, Dick

165.   Francis, Dick.   The Sport of Queens.   London: Michael
Joseph, 1957.   238p.   Illus.   Second revised edition, London:
Michael Joseph, 1974.   248p.   Illus. , index.   American
edition, New York: Harper and Row, 1969.   247p.   Illus. ,
index.

The first edition of Francis's book deals strictly with
his life before he became one of the finest writers of thrillers
of the past twenty years.   The biggest mystery covered in
the account of his career as a jockey is why the Queen
Mother's horse, Devon Loch, went down in a heap in the
stretch run of the 1956 Grand National.   Heart attack?
"Ghost" jump?   Muscle spasm?   Fear of crowd noise?   The
exciting style of the memoir foreshadows Francis's success
as a novelist.   A brief afterword in the American edition
includes an offhand mention of the novels, and an added chapter (pages 231-242) in the second revised British edition
covers his life since the Devon Loch episode (1957-1964),
including a little on his mystery writing and the end of his
riding career.

FREEMAN, R. Austin

166.   Donaldson, Norman.   In Search of Dr. Thorndyke:
The Story of R. Austin Freeman's Great Scientific Investigator
and his Creator.   Bowling Green, Ohio: Bowling Green University Popular Press, 1971.   xii, 288p.   Illus. , bibl. ,
index.

R. Austin Freeman has been somewhat devalued by
some recent commentators on the detective story, though
the hard-to-please Raymond Chandler was an admitted fan
of his work.   This very careful and scholarly biographical-
critical account is the only book on Freeman, but fortunately
it is a very thorough one.   Donaldson reprints in their en-
tirety many of Freeman's letters to his American friend and
promoter, Vincent Starrett, and he provides both a checklist
of Freeman's works and a descriptive bibliography.
Though he admits that Freeman's lack of interest in
reading other people's detective stories may have contributed
to his remaining resolutely old-fashioned, Donaldson compares
his subject favorably with many of his more flamboyant Golden
Age colleagues.

GARDNER, Erle Stanley

167. Fugate, Francis L. and Roberta B. Secrets of the World's Best-Selling Writer: The Storytelling Techniques of Erle Stanley Gardner. New York: Morrow, 1980. 286p. Illus. , bibl. , index.

Drawing on the collection of Gardner's papers at the University of Texas in Austin, the Fugates have produced one of the most fascinating books ever written about commercial fiction writing. Though the book is probably more instructive as an insight into Gardner and his work than as a how-to manual, prospective writers of fiction can learn much from the meticulousness and determination of Perry Mason's creator, who may have gone farther on less raw talent than any other writer in the mystery field. The book is full of insights on story construction, author-editor relations, the creation of series characters, plotting formulas, title selection, and numerous other problems faced by the Gardner fiction factory. Illustrations include photographs, pages from Gardner's plotting notebooks, a selection from the Perry Mason comic strip, and interior illustrations from Mason's magazine appearances. Several charts and outlines used by Gardner in constructing his plots are included in the appendixes, along with a Perry Mason title analysis (evoking such never-recorded novel possibilities as The Case of the Good-natured Hangman, The Case of the Negligent Chaperone, and The Case of the Colorblind Corpse). Selections from Gardner's last plotting notebook, covering the novels The Case of the Fabulous Fake and All Grass Isn't Green, give the lie to any suggestion that Gardner was resting on his laurels in the latter part of his writing career. The two-page bibliography lists Gardner's published articles on the techniques of writing.

168. Hughes, Dorothy B. Erle Stanley Gardner: The Case of the Real Perry Mason. New York: Morrow, 1978. 350p. Illus. , bibl. , index.

Here is a rare instance of one outstanding mystery novelist writing the biography of another; indeed, both are recipients of the Mystery Writers of America's Grand Master award. While this is a valuable book to have--it is unfailingly readable and presents more of the facts of Gardner's life than have appeared in print before--it is disappointing in some ways, more a eulogy or tribute than a true biography.

The greatest lack is any kind of assessment of Gardner's strengths and weaknesses as a writer, something Hughes as a longtime reviewer of mystery fiction might have been expected to provide. There is not even any admission of the decline of his later works.

A particular annoyance is the quoting of Gardner's strictly nonlibelous opinions of other writers without identifying who is being discussed. While it will be obvious to many readers that Craig Rice is the object of the discussion on page 210 (and the fact is discoverable by anyone who chooses to dig for it), she goes unidentified for no apparent reason.

A valuable bibliography of Gardner's books and magazine stories, compiled by Ruth Moore, is included.

169.   Johnston, Alva.   The Case of Erle Stanley Gardner. New York: Morrow, 1947.   87p.   Illus. , bibl.

The important point to make about this short profile of Gardner is that it is not superseded by Dorothy B. Hughes's biography.   There is discussion of the Perry Mason stories, especially their legal aspects, that is not covered by Hughes, including the use of The Case of the Curious Bride in a real-life murder trial.   The basic theme is how the lawyer Gardner was shaped the writer that he was to become.   No unrealistic claims are made for Gardner's literary stature--the book suggests just the kind of writer his novels reveal Gardner to be, and would certainly attract any legal-minded reader (if there were any) not already aware of the Mason novels.   With sixteen pages of photographs included in the page count, this is an even briefer book than might at first appear.

170.   Mundell, E. H.   Erle Stanley Gardner: A Checklist (The Serif Series: Bibliographies and Checklists, No. 6). Kent, Ohio: Kent State University Press, 1968.   91p.   Index.

Although the information it offers is less complete than might have been desired, this is a useful first stab at Gardner bibliography.   Listed in separate sections are short fiction (arranged by year and within the year by periodical), book fiction (by year, giving the place of publication only for foreign editions) through The Case of the Careless Cupid (1968), short nonfiction, book nonfiction, and miscellanea (including a very incomplete list of Gardner's magazine series characters and some of the titles of the stories in which they appear). The extremely sketchy indexes include keywords in titles (Bird, Candle, etc.), characters, pseudonyms, and nonfiction subjects.

GIBSON, Walter B.

171. Eisgruber, Frank, Jr. Gangland's Doom: The Shadow of the Pulps. Oak Lawn, Illinois: Robert Weinberg, 1974. 64p. Illus.

Not examined. In his bibliography in The Mystery Story (see #63), Robert E. Briney describes it as follows: "Exhaustive analysis of the pulp magazine novels about The Shadow, with more information than anyone but a fanatic could want ..." (page 381).

172. Gibson, Walter B. The Shadow Scrapbook. Preface by Chris Steinbrunner. Contributing editor: Anthony Tollin. New York: Harcourt Brace Jovanovich, 1979. v, 162p. Illus., bibl.

Gibson has written many accounts of the genesis of The Shadow, always somehow managing to tell the story in a slightly different way, but never more thoroughly than in this handsome large-format paperback. A selection of depictions of The Shadow in the covers of the pulp magazine bearing his name includes several in color. The screen, radio, comic-book, and paperback careers of the famous character are also covered. A feature of special reference interest is the listing of all Shadow radio shows, giving date, title, and script-writer when known. Among the well-known mystery writers to do Shadow scripts at one time or another were Max Ehrlich, Frank Kane, Robert Arthur, Alfred Bester, and John Roeburt. Other features of interest include the first Shadow radio script, a new "deductive" Shadow novelette by Gibson, and a full sequence from the short-lived Shadow comic strip.

173. Murray, Will. The Duende History of the Shadow Magazine. Greenwood, Massachusetts: Odyssey, 1980. 128p. Illus., bibl.

Some proofreading problems aside, this is a first-rate example of "fannish," as opposed to "academic," history.

The lead article identifies such diverse influences on the
Shadow novels as Horatio Alger, Maurice Leblanc, Alexandre
Dumas, Sherlock Holmes, Bulwer-Lytton, Bela Lugosi, and
Al Jolson. We also learn that author Gibson, like Frederic
Dannay of the Ellery Queen team, loves the Oz books.
Though this is ostensibly a history of the magazine, the em-
phasis is more on the development and history of the Shadow
character, and thus basically on Gibson. Only in Robert
Sampson's article, "The Third Cranston," does the focus
actually shift to the magazine, and then only very briefly
and in relation to the late-forties Shadow novels written by
Bruce Elliott. (To this reader, by the way, the Elliott
Shadows come out sounding more interesting than those by
Gibson or his usual second string "Maxwell Grant," Theodore
Tinsley. Won't someone please reprint them?) There is
generally more detail throughout on plots and characters than
most casual readers will want.

   Murray includes a checklist of Shadow novels, giving
published title, working title, date of submission, date of
publication, and author. Like Gibson's Shadow Scrapbook
(see #172), this volume includes a new Shadow story. There
are also interviews with Gibson and Tinsley.

   I can't resist quoting a textbook dangling modifier:
"Unlike Tinsley, Gibson's master villains are never permitted
to be female ..." (page 37).

GIELGUD, Val

174. Gielgud, Val. Years in a Mirror. London: The
Bodley Head, 1965. 224p. Index.

   Most of this memoir of the brother of Sir John Gielgud and longtime BBC radio-drama head deals with matters
other than his many detective novels, most of which have not
been published in the United States. They are referred to
briefly in a chapter about his writing career, which reveals
a certain irritation at being typed as a thriller writer.
Gielgud belongs to the decorous and reticent school of mem-
oirists rather than the let-it-all-hang-out-school.

175. Gielgud, Val. Years of the Locust. London: Nicolson
and Watson, 1947. viii, 206p. Illus.

   The first volume of autobiography by Gielgud includes
more on his early life, family background, childhood, school-

ing, World War I experiences, brother John, and early
theatrical career, but (if anything) even less about his mystery writing. There is, though, an account of appearing in
Edgar Wallace's The Ringer on stage, material on movie-
making (including the film version of Death at Broadcasting
House) , a reference to John Dickson Carr and his wartime
BBC series, "Appointment with Fear," and much discussion
of the production of radio plays, some criminous in nature.
Gielgud drops many names and quotes extensively from his
travel diaries, including one on the Hollywood of 1938.
Though the author comes off (despite his protestations to the
contrary) as a quintessential snob, the book is well written
and the opinions and prejudices more entertaining than most.

GRUBER, Frank

176. Clark, William J. The Frank Gruber Index. Los
Angeles: William J. Clark, 1969. 18p.

        Clark lists Gruber's books chronologically, including
exact publication date in most cases. Magazine stories are
listed by magazine title, then chronologically, with title,
number of pages when known, name of main character, and
pen name used where appropriate. Articles are listed by
magazine title in a separate section, including such diverse
periodicals as Hollywood Diary, The Leghorn World, and
Wayside Salesman. Gruber was still living at the time this
valuable bibliography was published, so some of his last
works are not included.

HAMMETT, Dashiell

177. Layman, Richard. Dashiell Hammett: A Descriptive
Bibliography (Pittsburgh Series in Bibliography). Pittsburgh:
University of Pittsburgh Press, 1979. xiii, 185p. Illus. ,
index.

        Like its companion piece on Raymond Chandler (see
#117), this is a fully descriptive bibliography, reproducing
title pages and dust jackets or covers of the first editions
of Hammett's books and listing later editions. Besides the
novels and short-story collections, there are such items as
the comic strip Secret Agent X-9 and the wartime pamphlet
The Battle of the Aleutians. Other sections note contributions to books, periodicals, and newspapers; public letters

and petitions signed by Hammett; and movie work (a surprisingly sparse listing). This is, of course, a cornerstone
volume for the collector.

178. Mundell, E. H. A List of the Original Appearances
of Dashiell Hammett's Magazine Work (The Serif Series:
Bibliographies and Checklists, No. 13). Kent, Ohio: Kent
State University Press, 1970. 52p.

Not examined. Although the listing includes material
not in Nolan's Casebook bibliography (see #179), the review
in Choice (December 1970, page 1360) pronounced this checklist inferior to Nolan's. Both are now superseded by Layman's bibliography (see #177).

179. Nolan, William F. Dashiell Hammett: A Casebook.
Introduction by Philip Durham. Santa Barbara, California:
McNally and Loftin, 1969. xvi, 189p. Bibl. , index.

This excellent biographical-critical account, written
without much cooperation from Lillian Hellman, guardian of
Hammett's papers, is the pioneering book-length study of
the Continental Op's chronicler and as of this writing the
only biography, though volumes by Diane Johnson (authorized)
and Richard Layman (not) are forthcoming. Though Nolan's
bibliography of Hammett's own work is now superseded by
Layman (see #177), the annotated bibliography of secondary
sources from books and periodicals remains most valuable.
Nolan's early spadework provides an important resource for
all future writers on Hammett.

180. Wolfe, Peter. Beams Falling: The Art of Dashiell
Hammett. Bowling Green, Ohio: Bowling Green University
Popular Press, 1980. 168p. Notes.

One of the more surprising points made in this superbly
written critical study of Hammett's output is the range of
elements that unite, rather than separate, Hammett and the
writers of classical detective fiction. Wolfe refers to Hammett's use of Queenian dying messages, his emphasis on
physical evidence, his use of Christie-like misdirection, and
his variations on Poe's "Purloined Letter" solution. Wolfe
points out, "Unlike Raymond Chandler, he wasn't undermining
the crime-puzzle tradition so much as extending it" (page 27).

Wolfe makes a strong case for Hammett's importance as a writer of short stories, ranking him with Fitzgerald and Hemingway. In fact, though he discusses each of the novels at length (giving first place to The Maltese Falcon), he seems to value the short stories more. The detail and the inference-drawing are extensive, but Hammett is a substantial enough writer to stand up to it without appearing ridiculous. There is never that impression of belaboring the obvious that often marks the overdone symbol-chasing of academic critics.

HIMES, Chester

181. Himes, Chester. The Quality of Hurt (The Autobiography of Chester Himes, Volume I). Garden City, New York: Doubleday, 1972. 351p. Illus.

182. Himes, Chester. My Life of Absurdity (The Autobiography of Chester Himes, Volume II). Garden City, New York: Doubleday, 1976. 398p. Illus., bibl.

The author of the Harlem detective novels about Coffin Ed Johnson and Grave-Digger Jones moved to Europe in the early fifties and is extremely bitter about the United States, as the reader is constantly reminded. Though Himes's profound anger is probably more effectively expressed indirectly through his fiction than it is here more explicitly, his story-telling skills do not fail him in the first volume of this autobiography. The second volume, which describes his entry into detective fiction, is less successful, overly detailed and marked by a tendency to quote in full letters of doubtful relevance that he wrote or received. Himes reveals that he once began a novel about black revolution called Plan B, in which Grave-Digger kills Coffin Ed.
At one point in volume two, Himes makes the statement, " ... I still felt as much of a stranger in Paris as I did in every white country I had ever been in; I only felt at home in my detective stories" (page 381).

183. Milliken, Stephen F. Chester Himes: A Critical Appraisal. Columbia: University of Missouri Press, 1976. 312p. Bibl.

This book made me want to chuck work and go read Himes's novels, thus passing the severest test of any critical study. Although he spends 46 pages on the Harlem detective novels about Coffin Ed and Grave-Digger, Milliken has a rather low opinion of detective fiction generally, making the statement, "Like most everything written for the subgenre, Himes's detective novels read as though they had been written with a possible film adaptation in mind" (page 215). This is both sweeping and sneering, as well as breathtakingly inaccurate. The chapter on the mysteries, though some of the comparisons with other writers seem doubtful, is basically excellent, with a judicious use of quotations to capture the unique flavor of Himes's work.

HOUSEHOLD, Geoffrey

184. Household, Geoffrey. Against the Wind. London: Michael Joseph, 1958. 238p. American edition, Boston: Little, Brown, 1958. 238p.

The autobiography of the British adventure-story writer best known for Rogue Male is divided into three sections: "Traveller," "Soldier," and "Craftsman." They are accurately named, the first section almost pure travelogue, the second (and longest) an account of his World War II experiences, and only the third (and shortest) a discussion of his career as a novelist.

He estimated his rank as a writer "equivalent to a wartime major-general--among, that is, the first two hundred, any of whom may as easily be retired to discomfort as advance to higher authority" (page 197). Though brief, his section on the writer's craft and his own development is beautifully expressed and cries out for quotation. "I try to present my goods to the passer-by with the clarity which politeness demands" (page 199). "With those first two novels my laborious method of working became standardised, and through the years has only gained in slowness. I cannot think that I am a natural writer at all" (page 209). Natural writer or not, Household is a stylist and a half.

LE FANU, Sheridan

185. Browne, Nelson. Sheridan Le Fanu. London: Arthur Barker, 1951. 135p. Bibl., index.

This is a brief, rather dry biographical-critical study of the author of Uncle Silas and an important figure in the

nineteenth-century development of the mystery-detective form.
Browne offers a brief chapter on what is known of Le Fanu's
life; chapters on the novels, short stories, and verse; and
a judicious summing up of the author's place in literature.

LE QUEUX, William

186. Le Queux, William. Things I Know About Kings,
Celebrities, and Crooks. London: Eveleigh Nash and Grayson, 1923. 320p. Illus., index.

     As the title suggests, this memoir is more devoted
to name-dropping anecdotes and reminiscences than true
autobiography. In the preface, Le Queux reprints his Who's
Who biography for readers interested in the bare facts of
his life. Though the prolific writer of thrillers has some
fine stories to tell, his reliability has often been called into
question.

187. Sladen, Norman St. Barbe. The Real Le Queux: The
Official Biography of William Le Queux. London: Nicolson
and Watson, 1938. xx, 239p. Illus.

     This volume may be a more reliable account of Le
Queux's life than Things I Know ... (see #186), but I have
not been able to run down a copy to examine. The British
Library copy is missing.

MACDONALD, John D.

188. Campbell, Frank D., Jr. John D. MacDonald and
the Colorful World of Travis McGee (The Milford Series:
Popular Writers of Today, Vol. 5). San Bernardino, California: R. Reginald/The Borgo Press, 1977. 63p. Bibl.

     The only critical monograph to date on MacDonald
ignores his many nonseries books to concentrate on his color-
coded series about Florida salvage consultant McGee. Campbell coverage extends through the sixteenth book in the
series, The Dreadful Lemon Sky (1975). Aside from a short
paragraph preceding the bibliography, there is no biographical
material here on MacDonald. The book-by-book summary
style is a bit monotonous, and the considerations are heavy
on the side of plot summary. Though Campbell admires

MacDonald, the tone of his summaries is irreverent and sometimes facetious. This pamphlet is recommended for readers whose favorite reference book is <u>Masterplots</u>.

189. Moffatt, Len and June, and William J. Clark. <u>The JDM Master Checklist: A Bibliography of the Published Writings of John D. MacDonald.</u> Downey, California: Moffatt House, 1969. xvii, 42p. Illus. , index.

    Putting together a complete bibliography of a writer as prolific as MacDonald seems a staggering task, made somewhat easier by the fact that he scorns the use of pseudonyms (though some of his early pulp stories were published under house names). This pamphlet didn't include all of MacDonald's work through the date of publication--the Moffatts issued additions and corrections for some time after with their periodical, <u>The JDM Bibliophile</u>--but it does go a long way toward that goal.
    Following a four-page biographical account, the bibliography is arranged in the following sections: American magazine stories and articles (arranged by periodical title and giving date, title, wordage or page count, and byline), stories in anthologies (chronologically), hardcover and paperback books in U.S. editions, special list of Fawcett editions with stock numbers (current as of 1969), British editions, British magazine appearances, and foreign editions. A title index is included.

MACDONALD, Ross (Kenneth Millar)

190. Bruccoli, Matthew. <u>Kenneth Millar/Ross Macdonald: A Checklist.</u> Introduction by Kenneth Millar. Detroit: Gale, 1971. xvii, 86p. Illus.

    The main section is a chronological bibliography of Millar/Macdonald first editions, with a reproduced title page on the left-hand page and bibliographic information (including listings of British and reprint editions) on the right. Novels cited range from <u>The Dark Tunnel</u> (1944) to <u>The Underground Man</u> (1971). Also included are lists of first book appearances of stories and essays, published short stories, articles, verse, book reviews, letters, blurbs, interviews, and miscellaneous references. The first pages of a couple of Millar's University of Michigan term papers are shown, plus entries in his notebooks for <u>The Galton Case</u>, <u>The Goodbye</u>

Look, and The Underground Man. The introduction is a
nice autobiographical piece, some but not all of the information familiar from other sources.

191. Macdonald, Ross. On Crime Writing (Yes! Capra
Chapbook Series, No. 11). Foreword by Noel Young. Santa
Barbara, California: Capra, 1973. vii, 45p.

Included are two previously published essays, "The
Writer as Detective Hero" and "Writing The Galton Case."
The first discusses Dupin, Holmes, Spade, and Marlowe,
comparing and contrasting them with Macdonald's own Lew
Archer. The second discusses the development of the novel
he felt marked a turning point in his writing career. The
foreword gives a brief but illuminating view of Macdonald
(Kenneth Millar) as a teacher of writing.

192. Speir, Jerry. Ross Macdonald (Recognitions: Detec-
tive/Suspense). New York: Ungar, 1978. ix, 182p. Bibl.,
index.

The second monograph about Macdonald, including a
chapter of biography followed by a critical summary of all
the novels through The Blue Hammer (1976), is less dense
than Wolfe's (see #193) and thus probably more accessible
to the general reader. It, too, may be overdevoted to plot
summary for many readers, however. Speir believes The
Underground Man to be Macdonald's best. After the chronological summary, separate chapters discuss the character
of Archer, Macdonald's themes, his style, and his overall
achievement. The excellent five-page bibliography includes
both primary and secondary sources.

193. Wolfe, Peter. Dreamers Who Live Their Dreams:
The World of Ross Macdonald's Novels. Bowling Green,
Ohio: Bowling Green University Popular Press, 1976. 346p.
Notes, index.

This is an extremely detailed examination of Ross
Macdonald's career in every aspect. It is so exhaustive
that it becomes very slow reading. Telling points are made,
though, and Macdonald's work merits such serious treatment.
Unlike some academics who write about the private-eye big
three, Wolfe seems fairly well acquainted with other detective

fiction. Those intimidated by the overwhelming detail of
academic criticism will find the chapter on Archer's character a delight before the overwhelming plot summaries have
a chance to lose them.

MACLEAN, Alistair

194. Lee, Robert A. Alistair MacLean: The Key Is Fear
(The Milford Series: Popular Writers of Today, Vol. 2).
San Bernardino, California: R. Reginald/The Borgo Press,
1976. 60p. Bibl.

This pamphlet represents pure literary criticism,
jumping right into a consideration of H. M. S. Ulysses, Mac-
Lean's first book, with no attempt at providing a biographical context. As the only monograph on MacLean, this volume
has some value, though it is written in unexciting prose,
lacks profundity of observation, and fails the ultimate test:
it does not make the reader want to rush off and read Mac-
Lean. Lee does a particular disservice to his subject in
the passages he quotes. MacLean is an undistinguished
stylist never seen at his best when quoted out of context.
Though MacLean is probably worthy of this kind of extended
treatment, Lee never really suggests why. Finally, he reveals solutions for no good reason.

MARSH, Ngaio

195. Marsh, Ngaio. Black Beech and Honeydew: An Autobiography. London: Collins, 1966. 287p. Illus. American
edition, Boston: Little, Brown, 1965. 343p. Illus.

Although it is to her fame as a detective novelist that
Marsh owes the publication of this memoir, she spends disappointingly little space discussing her work in that field
and much more on her work in the theater, equally important
perhaps but less widely known. She describes the creation
of her first novel in an offhand way, not even mentioning
its title, and seems almost regretful that she took up writing
detective fiction as a life's pursuit. There is some interesting material, though, about the theatrical version of her
third book, The Nursing Home Murder, written with Dr.
Henry Jellet. Occasionally, there is passing reference to
whatever mystery novel she was working on at a particular
time, but little else.

MASON, A. E. W.

196. Green, Roger Lancelyn. <u>A. E. W. Mason</u>. London: Max Parrish, 1952. 272p. Illus., bibl., index.

Though actor-dramatist-novelist Mason may be best known for the famous adventure novel <u>The Four Feathers</u>, he made an important contribution to detective fiction in his creation of Hanaud, the detective of <u>At the Villa Rose</u>, <u>The House of the Arrow</u>, and other novels. In this biographical-critical account of Mason's career, Green tells much about the origins of the characters and plots in the Hanaud novels, including a reading of Hanaud's characteristics in Mason himself (shades of Holmes and Conan Doyle). Unlike most other commentators, Green thinks <u>They Wouldn't Be Chessmen</u> (1935) was the best Hanaud novel, and he considers <u>The Witness for the Defence</u> (1913), a nonseries novel first written as a play, "one of the best tales of mystery and adventure that Mason ever wrote" (page 128).

OPPENHEIM, E. Phillips

197. Oppenheim, E. Phillips. <u>The Pool of Memory</u>. London: Hodder and Stoughton, 1941. ix, 300p. Illus., index. American edition, Boston: Little, Brown, 1942. vii, 341p. Illus.

The autobiography of the prolific thriller-writer is a desultory, anecdotal, name-dropping account with practically nothing about his work. There is much dialogue, either invention or a tribute to the author's prodigious memory. The latter part concerns his return to England from his home on the French Riviera at the outbreak of World War II.

198. Standish, Robert. <u>The Prince of Storytellers: The Life of E. Phillips Oppenheim</u>. London: Peter Davies, 1957. 253p. Bibl.

Despite a rather bitchy tone, this is one of the most lively and readable mystery-writer biographies. Identifying <u>The Pool of Memory</u> (see #197) as Oppenheims worst book, a product of fading memory and ill-conceived selectivity, Standish ultimately conveys pretty well what sort of man Oppenheim was as well as the reasons for the appeal of his books. Some passages suggest that Standish shares his subject's anti-Semitism, homophobia, and (not surprisingly) sexism. There are many references to Oppy's philandering, understandably not referred to in the autobiography. Standish describes his subject as "an amazing mixture of hedonist and puritan" (page 99). He presents an extremely unattractive picture of the phony-ridden Riviera society in which Oppy spent most of the second half of his life. One chapter discusses the specific sums of money paid for some of Oppenheim's fiction--Nicholas Goade, Detective realized $21,965.54 in the United States and £1,484, 15s. in Britain. The initial series was written in less than two months in 1925.

The main problems here are an occasional sense of the biographer struggling with a shortage of hard data and a disappointing lack of information about the content of Oppenheim's books.

ORCZY, Baroness

199. Orczy, Baroness. Links in the Chain of Life. London: Hutchinson, n. d. (1947). 223p. Illus., index.

There is much about the Scarlet Pimpernel in this chatty autobiography, but very little on the armchair detective of the author's short stories, The Old Man in the Corner. The Baroness does record, however, the stir she created by having a coroner's inquest in a story laid in Scotland, where there is no such thing.

POST, Melville Davisson

200. Norton, Charles A. Melville Davisson Post: Man of Many Mysteries. Bowling Green, Ohio: Bowling Green University Popular Press, 1973. 261p. Illus., bibl., index.

Norton advances the thesis that the identification of Post, the creator of "criminal-lawyer" Randolph Mason and Uncle Abner, as a mystery writer is "as totally unfair as it is damaging. Much of what he wrote, even when it bordered on the mystery and detective field of interest, does not belong there, and some of the best things he wrote are clearly outside of that division" (page 5). The only full-length book on Post, about one-fourth biography and three-fourths criticism, offers a thorough consideration of an unjustly neglected figure in American literature. However, it also has severe problems: a drab cover, a lead-footed writing style, much repetition, and what may be a world's record for dangling and misplaced modifiers. Much of this could have been corrected by a good editor. Another problem is the constant reference to photographs not reproduced in the book. There is no picture here of Mrs. Post and no recognizable likeness of Post himself. (I know one exists: it appears in Haycraft's Murder for Pleasure, see #1.)

QUEEN, Ellery (Frederic Dannay and Manfred B. Lee)

201. Nevins, Francis M., Jr. Royal Bloodline: Ellery Queen, Author and Detective. Bowling Green, Ohio: Bowling Green University Popular Press, 1974. 288p. Illus., bibl., index.

While Agatha Christie and Dorothy L. Sayers have been written about excessively, this is the only book-length study of the greatest American proponents of the classical detective story. Fortunately, it is an excellent one, principally a critical history of the works of Frederic Dannay and Manfred B. Lee under the names of Queen and Barnaby Ross, with only a few biographical details included. In addition to the team's novels and short stories, Nevins discusses the team's radio work, the motion pictures made from their novels, and the contributions of Queen (primarily the Dannay half) as editor, anthologist, scholar, and bibliographer. Nevins examines the Queen works both for their detective-story content (with an especially keen eye for plotting lacunae) and for their deeper thematic implications. Nevins proves that it is possible to do meaningful criticism of detective stories without routinely giving away the endings. He will reveal a solution if it's absolutely vital for a point he is making--as in the discussion of The Last Woman in His Life--but not without warning the reader in advance. There should be a book like this about every major writer of detective fiction, but only Robert Barnard's A Talent to Deceive (see #127) on Agatha Christie is really comparable. An excellent selection of photographs is included. An Ellery Queen checklist is divided into three parts: fiction (both in books and periodicals), editorial and critical work, and association items. The latter section includes a list of selected writings about Queen.

RINEHART, Mary Roberts

202. Cohn, Jan. Improbable Fiction: The Life of Mary

Roberts Rinehart. Pittsburgh: University of Pittsburgh
Press, 1980. xv, 293p. Illus. , bibl. , index.

Drawing on unpublished autobiographical writings produced late in Rinehart's life, Cohn provides a corrective to
the "Rinehart myth" presented in My Story (see #203) and
other writings about the prolific author. Both the biographical and critical content are impressive, though Cohn gives
more attention to Rinehart's mainstream fiction and nonfiction magazine articles than to her mysteries, surprising
from a writer who early on expresses her longtime interest
in writing a biography of a mystery writer. The chronological bibliography offers a fascinating feature: the price Rinehart was paid for each item, as well as its title, date, and
place of publication.

203. Rinehart, Mary Roberts. My Story. New York:
Farrar and Rinehart, 1931. vi, 432p. Illus. Revised
edition, New York: Rinehart, 1948. 570p. illus.

Though she is out of fashion today, there is a magic
to Rinehart's prose that is evident from the early stages of
her autobiography. She juxtaposes everyday events with
sudden and shocking violent ones in the manner of one of
her mystery novels. Beneath what seems like rosy-lensed
nostalgia, the real world never seems hidden for long. Very
few of the gothicists of the sixties and since can match her
as a stylist. And her views--ecologically, educationally,
and socially--seem remarkably modern fifty years after she
put them on paper. Though there are many details of her
personal life Rinehart does not choose to discuss--some of
them revealed in Cohn's biography (see #202)--there is an
impression throughout this volume of a woman being painfully
honest with herself and her readers.

ROHMER, Sax (Arthur Henry Sarsfield Ward)

204. Van Ash, Cay, and Elizabeth Sax Rohmer. Master of
Villainy. Edited, with Foreword, Notes, and Bibliography,
by Robert E. Briney. Bowling Green, Ohio: Bowling Green
University Popular Press, 1972. ix, 312p. Illus. , bibl. ,
index.

By the evidence of this biography, the creator of Fu
Manchu truly inhabited a Sax Rohmer world of opium dens,
mysterious seductresses, haunted houses, sinister Oriental

villains, and occult phenomena. Though signed by the widow and a friend and protégé of the famed thriller-writer, the book was planned in Rohmer's lifetime, and parts of it were written by him. Not too surprisingly, the authors inflate Rohmer's importance as a writer beyond all reason, but the book is well written and as action-packed as one of its subject's novels. Briney's bibliography and notes add valuable scholarly support to the work.

SAYERS, Dorothy L.

205. Dale, Alzina Stone. Maker and Craftsman: The Story of Dorothy L. Sayers. Grand Rapids, Michigan: Eerdmans, 1978. xiv, 158p. Illus.

Though there is nothing in this book or on its jacket that specifically identifies it as a juvenile, it was clearly written for a very unsophisticated audience. It is a responsible enough biography, but the simplified language and the obvious attempt to counter the sensationalism of Janet Hitchman's controversial Such a Strange Lady (see #211) render it rather drab and bland. Dale has the unfortunate habit of unnecessarily throwing in the adjective "famous" at frequent intervals, and she makes some mistakes that will annoy mystery buffs, such as a reference to "Freeman Croft Wills" and an implication that Ellery Queen's Mystery Magazine existed in the twenties.

206. Durkin, Mary Brian, O. P. Dorothy L. Sayers (Twayne's English Authors Series, No. 281). Boston: Twayne, 1980. 204p. Illus. , bibl. , index.

In a book starting with two strikes against it--it concerns a writer who lately has been discussed and analyzed to death, and it has to conform to the rigid format of the Twayne series--Sister Durkin does a commendable job. Spending slightly more than half the book discussing the detective fiction (probably about right), she provides the most satisfactory critical commentary on Sayers as an author of mysteries of any of the book-length writers. She spends more time on the short stories than do other commentators. Though she frequently reveals the endings of the novels, she withholds them in discussing some of Sayers's best short stories, such as "Suspicion" and "The Man Who Knew How." Durkin also discusses Sayers's anthologies and her part in the Detection Club collaborative novels. The annotated bibliography of secondary sources is excellent and right up to date.

207. Gilbert, Colleen B. A Bibliography of the Works of Dorothy L. Sayers. Hamden, Connecticut: Archon, 1978. 263p. Illus., index.

This fully descriptive bibliography is a magnificent achievement, made more difficult (according to the introduction) by Sayers's own failure to keep her bibliographic records straight and by the destruction of some periodical backruns during World War II. The entries are divided into the following categories, arranged chronologically and numbered within each: A--books, pamphlets, cards, and ephemera by D.L.S. alone or in collaboration (with some covers and title pages reproduced); B--contributions to books, pamphlets, and miscellanea; C--contributions to newspaper and periodicals; D--book reviews; E--broadcasts, play productions, films, and records (published and unpublished); and G--manuscript collections. Section D includes lists of the authors and titles of the many mysteries reviewed by Sayers in a weekly London Sunday Times column between 1933 and 1935. These seem a prime candidate for reprinting--as do the mystery reviews of Dashiell Hammett and Dylan Thomas, while we're at it.

208. Hall, Trevor H. Dorothy L. Sayers: Nine Literary Studies. London: Duckworth, 1980. xi, 132p. Illus., index. American edition, Hamden, Connecticut: Archon, 1980. 132p. Illus., index.

One of the more entertaining analysts of the Holmes saga turns his attention to the life and work of Sayers in a book mostly devoted to genuine (if arcane) literary detective work, not mock scholarship in the Sherlockian vein. Of particular interest are the chapters on Sayers's collaborator, "Robert Eustace," and on the life and career of Sayers's husband, Atherton Fleming. Other subjects include the influence of Conan Doyle on Sayers; the only non-Wimsey Sayers novel, The Documents in the Case; the chicken-or-egg provenance of the stage and novel versions of Busman's Honeymoon; and Sayers's attitude toward psychical research, another pet subject of Hall. The book has the distinction among Sayers studies of dealing wholly with the detective output, with barely a nod toward her Dante translations and religious dramas.

209.   Hannay, Margaret P. , ed.   As Her Whimsey Took Her: Critical Essays on the Work of Dorothy L. Sayers. Kent, Ohio: Kent State University Press, 1979.   xvi, 301p. Bibl. , index.

The first five essays in this volume (pages 1-64) deal with Sayers's detective fiction.   The remaining ten deal with aspects of her drama, translations, and aesthetics. The bibliographic section (pages 215-278), describing "Dorothy L. Sayers's Manuscripts and Letters in Public Collections in the United States," is the most valuable feature for scholars.
The detection-related essays are a well-written and challenging group, including R. B. Reaves on "Crime and Punishment in the Detective Fiction of Dorothy L. Sayers," R. D. Stock and Barbara Stock on "The Agents of Evil and Justice ... " in the novels, Lionel Basney on The Nine Tailors, editor Hannay on Harriet Vane's influence on Lord Peter's characterization, and E. R. Gregory on Sayers and Wilkie Collins.   Hannay and Gregory, along with Joe R. Christopher and R. Russell Maylone, compiled the bibliography.

210.   Harmon, Robert B. , and Margaret A. Burger.   An Annotated Guide to the Works of Dorothy L. Sayers (Garland Reference Series in the Humanities, Vol. 80).   New York: Garland, 1977.   286p.   Illus. , index.

Not examined.   Donna J. McColman, writing in American Reference Books Annual 1978, calls this "a well-balanced and complete listing of Sayers's works in both the scholarly realm and the world of detective fiction.... Arrangement is by type of work and then alphabetically within the groupings....   The lengthy annotations give the flavor of the work. Annotations of Sayers's letters on a wide range of topics are fascinating in and of themselves and are generally more complete than book annotations....   This extremely well-done bibliography should set the standard for research on Dorothy Sayers for some time to come" (page 603).

211.   Hitchman, Janet.   Such a Strange Lady: An Introduction to Dorothy L. Sayers (1893-1957).   London: New English

Library, 1975. 203p. Illus., bibl. American edition, with subtitle A Biography of Dorothy L. Sayers, New York: Harper and Row, 1975. xiv, 177p. Illus., bibl.

The pioneering Sayers biography stresses the personal over the literary but seems rather thin on facts and long on rumor, speculation, and tangential discussions. The change in subtitle from the British to the American edition is instructive--the book is not a full-scale biography, and the author seems to realize it. In a readable, lively, sketchy work, Hitchman has captured Sayers the eccentric but given far less impression of her value and importance than do later works, particularly Ralph Hone's (see #212). Critical comments are superficial, and the bibliography is a spare checklist of the subject's books.

212. Hone, Ralph. Dorothy L. Sayers: A Literary Biography. Kent, Ohio: Kent State University Press, 1979. xvii, 217p. Illus., notes, index.

This is the best Sayers biography--scholarly (unlike Hitchman [see #211]) and written for adults (unlike Dale [see #205]). It gives an impression of Sayers as a fine and noble woman, with little suggestion of the zany eccentric that emerges from Hitchman's account. Whether the book really captures Sayers as a personality is doubtful, but it is a sound account of her life and works. The critical sections on the detective novels are less consistent and detailed than they might be--Hone apparently has more interest in her theological writings. This book won the Mystery Writers of America Edgar award for 1979 in the biographical-critical category.

213. Scott-Giles, C. W. The Wimsey Family: A Fragmentary History Compiled from Correspondence with Dorothy L. Sayers. London: Gollancz, 1977. 88p. Illus. American edition, New York: Harper and Row, 1977. 88p. Illus.

The author, in the same spirit that inspires the scholars of Sherlock Holmes, began in the thirties to ruminate on the family history of Lord Peter Wimsey. He wrote to Sayers, who joined in the game wholeheartedly, and the result is this work of mock-heraldry. Genealogy buffs may find the whole thing amusing.

SIMENON, Georges

214. Becker, Lucille Frackman. Georges Simenon (Twayne's World Author Series, No. 456). Boston: Twayne, 1977. 171p. Illus., bibl., index.

In a careful and readable general critical study of Simenon's writings, Becker devotes one chapter (pages 35-53) to the Maigret detective novels, incidentally crediting Balzac rather than Poe with the invention of the genre. The text refers to the novels by their French titles, though the English versions are included in the bibliography. Becker stresses the ways in which Simenon differs from most writers of detective fiction, how his interest in the motivation of the criminal outweighs his interest in creating a whodunit. The result is both a denigration of detective fiction and an underrating of Simenon as a builder of puzzle plots. Not surprisingly in treating a writer so prolific, Becker deals with the Maigret novels and Simenon's other work topically rather than chronologically. As usual with Twayne volumes, the bibliography of primary and secondary sources is very useful, though there should be an easier way to identify the French title with its English translation than browsing through a chronological list.

215. Courtine, Robert J. Madame Maigret's Recipes. Translated from the French by Mary Manheim. Preface by Georges Simenon. New York: Harcourt Brace Jovanovich, 1975. 183p. Illus.

Approaching the Maigrets as real people, this volume is more of a traditional cookbook than a commentary on the Maigret novels. Short quotations from the novels precede the recipes, which are logically arranged into categories: soups, sauces, entrées, eggs, fish, game, and so forth, finishing logically with desserts. Courtine frequently notes what wine Maigret drank with a given dish. The lack of a separate list of ingredients at the beginning of the recipe hampers the book's usefulness somewhat, according to my cookbook consultant.

216. Narcejac, Thomas. The Art of Simenon. Translated from the French by Cynthia Rowland. London: Routledge and Kegan Paul, 1952. vii, 178p. Bibl.

Narcejac makes an odd claim on the first page of this well-written and learned study. Is (or was) Maigret really "better known than Sherlock Holmes or Charlie Chaplin" even in France, let alone the whole world as Narcejac believes? The author's categorization of Simenon readers is amusing. He discusses the way in which Simenon's extreme prolificacy and his identification with the detective story have limited his critical acceptance as an important novelist. He goes on to make the provocative denial that Simenon ever wrote a detective story; his efforts to defend this assertion, while interesting, assume too narrow a definition of detective story to satisfy most devotees and serve to make him seem almost as unfriendly to the form as Edmund Wilson (see #85).

217. Raymond, John. Simenon in Court. London: Hamish Hamilton, 1968. xiii, 193p. Illus. , bibl.

The author of this first Simenon study to be written in English claims to have read about half of Simenon's fiction, in itself enough to keep a fast reader busy for a year or two. Paying greater attention to the author's nondetective writings (while constantly comparing him to Balzac), Raymond devotes one chapter ("The Mender of Destinies," pages 153-167) strictly to the Maigret tales. Appropriately, the chapter, heavy with quotations, is more a character sketch of Maigret than a critical history of his career. Raymond properly refers to the novels by their original French titles, with a chronological list in the appendix identifying the translations. As with Becker (see #214), there is provided no easier way to locate the novels by English title. Worse yet, there is no index.

218. Simenon, Georges. When I Was Old. Translated from the French by Helen Eustis. New York: Harcourt Brace Jovanovich, 1971. 343p. Illus. (French title: Quand j'étais vieux.)

The three notebooks published here were kept by Simenon between June 1960 and March 1962, a time when he was nearing sixty and beginning to feel his age. When he stopped feeling old, he says in his preface, he no longer felt "the need to write in notebooks, and those that I did not use I've given to my children." The product has some of the characteristics of a journal or of memoirs, but Simenon denies the intention to produce either. It is a work of painfully honest self-examination, offering much insight into Simenon the man and the writer, his aims, his methods, his problems, and his self-doubts. Not surprisingly, Simenon on Simenon proves more diverting than anyone else on Simenon.

219. Young, Trudee. George Simenon: A Checklist of His "Maigret" and Other Mystery Novels and Short Stories in French and in English Translations (The Scarecrow Author Bibliographies, No. 29). Metuchen, New Jersey: Scarecrow, 1976. 153p. Index.

This is undoubtedly the fullest bibliography of Simenon novels available in English. The novels are presented chronologically by their original French publication date. All French editions and English-language translations are listed. The subtitle notwithstanding, the listing includes nonmysteries by Simenon, though his pseudonymous apprentice writings have been omitted. Indexes to French and English titles are included, making it easier for the reader to identify the translated title with original than in most of the critical studies on Simenon. Young also offers a brief biographical sketch and references to sources of biographical and bibliographic information.

STOUT, Rex

220. Baring-Gould, William S. Nero Wolfe of West Thirty-Fifth Street: The Life and Times of America's Largest Private Detective. New York: Viking, 1969. xviii, 203p. Bibl.

The author of an earlier detective biography, Sherlock Holmes of Baker Street, attempts the same kind of thing on Rex Stout's orchid-growing sleuth--with entertaining results. The main difference between the two books is that here Baring-Gould sticks pretty much to the evidence in the Wolfe stories rather than inventing facts out of whole cloth as he did for Holmes. (That he was working here with the creation of a living author may have made the difference.) The final feature is a chronology of Wolfe's life and cases, beginning with his birth in 1892 or 1893 and continuing through The Father Hunt, which occurred in 1967 and was published in book form in 1968. One of Wolfe's book-length cases, The Second Confession, is unaccountably left out of the chronology.

221. McAleer, John. Rex Stout: A Biography. Foreword by P. G. Wodehouse. Boston: Little, Brown, 1977. xvi, 621p. Illus. , bibl. , index.

I think this large volume has the distinction of being the longest and most detailed biography ever written about a person chiefly regarded as mystery writer. Begun in the last years of Stout's life with its subject's full cooperation, the book covers every aspect of Nero Wolfe's creator and his writings in entertaining and scholarly fashion. Few lives are important and eventful enough to support this kind of extended biographical treatment, but Stout's was. Although the portrait McAleer presents is justifiably admiring, the few less attractive aspects of Stout's personality are not glossed over. Included are a fine selection of photographs, an excellent bibliography of writings by and about Stout, and 44 pages of notes that are often as fascinating reading as the biography itself. This volume won the Mystery Writers of America Edgar award as best biographical-critical study of 1977.

222. Stout, Rex. The Nero Wolfe Cook Book. Foreword by Fritz Brenner. New York: Viking, 1973. xv, 203p. Index.

Here is a mystery-oriented cookbook that had to happen--the only surprise is that it took as long as it did. The author credit reads "by Rex Stout and the editors of the Viking Press." In an acknowledgment at the beginning, Stout credits some of the latter by name and notes that only the quotes from the stories are wholly his. The table of contents shows more of a mystery than a cookbook orientation--the first few chapters deal logically with breakfast, lunch, dinner, and dessert, but chapters thereafter are keyed to features of the books: the relapse, Fritz Brenner, Rusterman's Restaurant, the Kanawha Spa dinner. Generous quotations from the books are included among the recipes. The instructions on the recipes are preceded by a list of ingredients, making them easier to use than those in the Madame Maigret cookbook (see #215).

TEY, Josephine (Elizabeth Mackintosh)

223. Roy, Sandra. Josephine Tey (Twayne's English Authors Series, No. 277). Boston: Twayne, 1980. 199p. Bibl., index.

Elizabeth Mackintosh considered her plays written as Gordon Daviot her most important works, but Roy's focus is on the better-known mystery novels that she wrote as Josephine Tey. Though this is a critical study rather than a biography, it becomes clear early that astonishingly little is known about the subject's life.

Roy offers detailed plot summaries, indeed more detailed than ideal in the interest of readability, and does not hesitate to reveal solutions. A minor theme is that Tey bridged the classical school of Sayers and Marsh and the hardboiled school of Hammett and Chandler. The structure of the book often seems overelaborated and too obviously outlined, but the quotes from Tey's work are well chosen and give a good idea of her charm as a writer. The obligatory book-by-book discussions of symbol and theme often belabor the obvious. Take for example Roy's statement that "things are not what they seem" and "appearances are deceiving" are continuing themes of Tey's work (page 180). Of what writer of mystery and detection are these not continuing themes? Do they really need repeated stating?

Thorough without being profound, this book is at least a valuable starting point in Tey scholarship.

UPFIELD, Arthur W.

224. Hawke, Jessica. Follow My Dust: A Biography of Arthur W. Upfield. Introduction by Detective Inspector Napoleon Bonaparte. London: Heinemann, 1957. xii, 238p. Illus.

Present here are two characteristics that reduce a reader's confidence in a popular biography: quite a bit of fiction-style dialogue and a paucity of dates, especially early on. Most of the book deals with Upfield's life before the beginning of his writing career--he arrives at the idea of mystery writing on page 167. There is interesting material here about the development of mystery plots peculiar to the Australian bush, including an account of the original method of body disposal in Upfield's The Sands of Windee and its employment in a real-life murder case.

VAN DINE, S. S. (Willard Huntington Wright)

225. Tuska, Jon, et al. <u>Philo Vance: The Life and Times</u> of S. S. Van Dine (Popular Writers Series, No. 1). Bowling Green, Ohio: Bowling Green University Popular Press, 1971. 63p. Illus. , bibl.

This pamphlet is the only monograph to date about one of the most significant and popular authors of detective novels of the twenties and thirties. Tuska's article, "The Philo Vance Murder Case," a résumé of the life of Van Dine (Willard Huntington Wright) and a critical history of the twelve novels about Vance, comprises slightly more than half of the pamphlet. Tuska makes some reference to the films about Vance, and the remaining three items (articles by Leonard Maltin and David R. Smith and a filmography by Karl Thiede) all concern the movies, giving Vance's cinematic career a somewhat disproportionate emphasis. Most interesting is Smith's article, "S. S. Van Dine at Twentieth Century-Fox," about the planning of a mystery vehicle for Sonja Henie.
    Though given to sweeping generalizations on occasion and marked by its author's usual pompous and pretentious style (and his tendency to give away solutions), the Tuska piece is a generally good survey. Van Dine is an author who deserves a fuller book-length treatment, both biographically and critically.

WALLACE, Edgar

226. Curtis, Robert G. <u>Edgar Wallace--Each Way.</u> London: John Long, n. d. (1932). 254p. Illus.

Wallace's longtime secretary and racecourse companion presents his reminiscences of his boss, including entertaining accounts of his unorthodox working methods; his gambling compulsion and financial profligacy; his odd habits of grammar, punctuation, and pronunciation (the latter rendering his Dictaphone recordings transcribable only by Curtis or Mrs. Wallace); and his vacillating political views. Curtis nominates <u>The Fellowship of the Frog</u> as Wallace's best and says the author concurred. There are chapters on Wallace's stage and film careers, his religious views, and his enthusiasm for horseracing--Curtis calls Wallace "the world's worst tipster." He also explodes the view (popular during his life) that Wallace was himself a good detective. Making no pretense of full-dress biography, this remains a very enjoyable memoir.

227. Lane, Margaret. Edgar Wallace: The Biography of a Phenomenon. London: Heinemann, n. d. (1938). xiii, 423p. Illus. , index.

This is the standard biography of the famed English thriller writer, highly readable and entertaining and illustrated with a fine selection of photographs. Details of Wallace's working methods and finances are numerous, but no critical analysis of his writings is attempted.

228. Lofts, W. O. G. , and Derek Adley. The British Bibliography of Edgar Wallace. Preface by Leslie Charteris. Introduction by Penelope Wallace. London: Howard Baker, 1969. 246p.

This is a painstaking job of tracking down all the books and periodical appearances of one of the most prolific writers of crime fiction. The two main sections list all the books alphabetically, noting first and reprint editions and dates and places of original magazine publications; and periodical stories and major articles listed by the title of the magazine or newspaper. In the latter section, the information is admittedly incomplete due to the rarity of many of the publications to which Wallace contributed. Also, some of his ephemeral writings have been omitted. Other listings include the books arranged by year of publication, untraced short stories, classification of first editions (describing and including the dedication to each book), collections of stories, appearances in anthologies, plays in collections, and true crime.

229. Wallace, Edgar. People. London: Hodder and Stoughton, n. d. (1926). 253p. American edition, Garden City, New York: Doubleday, Doran, for the Crime Club, 1929. xix, 234p.

As might be expected, Wallace's own account of his life is lively, anecdotal, uninformative about dates, and full of provocative opinions. The writing of his first mystery, The Four Just Men, is not discussed until page 180 (of the American edition) , as his early life fills most of the space available. There is very little about his writing thereafter. The American edition includes an introduction, "Edgar Wallace--the Legend," signed by "A. P. C."

230. Wallace, Ethel V. Edgar Wallace by His Wife. London: Hutchinson, n. d. (1932). 287p. Illus., index.

Here is one of two books of reminiscences to appear in 1932 by secretaries of Wallace--this one was also his wife. As with Robert G. Curtis's book (see #226), there is no attempt at a real biography here. Mrs. Wallace covers similar ground in a rather wandering, desultory fashion. There are numerous lengthy quotes from Wallace's letters. The emphasis on Wallace's family life and his relations with his children sets this apart from Curtis's work, but generally it is a far less engaging memoir.

WELLS, Carolyn

231. Wells, Carolyn. The Rest of My Life. Philadelphia: Lippincott, 1937. 395p. Illus., index.

This chatty, informal, free-associating item is more like a commonplace book than an autobiography. The gimmick is that Wells would tell what she was going to do with the rest of her life rather than look back. There are scattered mystery references to be found, but their sparseness is disappointing. There is only one page reference in the index to Fleming Stone, and the mention does not even make it clear that he was Wells's detective character. She describes meetings with Edgar Wallace and Israel Zangwill (who refused to talk about The Big Bow Mystery) and calls Eden Phillpotts the "author of the best detective stories written today" (page 15). She says of her pioneering volume The Technique of the Mystery Story (see #99), "anyone who reads it can learn by eye how to write detective stories as good as mine" (page 159). She then quotes a laudatory review by S. S. Van Dine.

WHEATLEY, Dennis

232. Hedman, Iwan, and Jan Alexandersson. Fyra Decennier med Dennis Wheatley (DAST Dossier, No. 1). Introduction by Lars Nylander. Strängnäs, Sweden: DAST, 1974. 192p. Illus., bibl.

Though some of the text of this volume is in Swedish, the unique descriptive bibliography of Wheatley first editions, the numerous illustrations, and a selection of Wheatley letters to author Hedman and others make this a useful volume for English-speaking readers. The title translates as Four Decades with Dennis Wheatley. Nylander's introduction is in both English and Swedish.

Wheatley, Dennis. The Time Has Come ... : The Memoirs of Dennis Wheatley.

233. The Young Man Said, 1897-1914. London: Hutchinson, 1977. 255p. Illus. , index.

234. Officer and Temporary Gentleman, 1914-1919. London: Hutchinson, 1978. 254p. Illus. , index.

235. Drink and Ink, 1919-1977. London: Hutchinson, 1979. 278p. Illus. , index.

Wheatley always believed in not shortchanging his readers in verbiage, thus this multivolume autobiography, originally envisioned for five volumes but cut down to three by Wheatley's declining health. The first two volumes barely get him through World War I and into his early twenties. The material about his writing career (as well as his career as a wine merchant) is concentrated in the third and final volume, which omits part of the account of his World War II experience for separate publication outside the memoirs.
Wheatley does not come across as a likable character. He exudes elitism, snobbishness, and conceit. All that said, he is a conscientious writer and a natural storyteller, and his memoirs include much material of interest.   †

† ADDENDUM

The four additional titles covered below bring What About
Murder? up to date, as nearly as possible, through the end
of 1980. Much activity in the field continues, although the
same writers who have been dealt with most frequently in the
past continue to monopolize most of the attention.
      Ungar has announced new critical works on Dorothy L.
Sayers (by Dawson Gaillard) and Raymond Chandler (by Jerry
Speir). Biographies of Dashiell Hammett by Richard Layman
and Diane Johnson are known to be in the works, though exact
publication dates have not been announced. Bill Pronzini's Gun
in Cheek, the first full-length study avowedly devoted to the
appreciation of bad detective fiction, is expected to see publication in 1981. Farther in the future is a much-needed biographical-critical study of Cornell Woolrich, a current project
of Francis M. Nevins, Jr.
      Two publishers have announced bibliographies of second-
ary sources on mystery fiction. Greenwood Press slated for
November 1980 publication David and Ann Skene Melvin's
Crime, Espionage, Mystery, and Thriller Fiction and Film:
A Comprehensive Bibliography of Critical Writing Through
1979, but no copy was available at press time. Garland has
scheduled for April 1981 publication Timothy and Julia Johnson's bibliography Crime Fiction Criticism.

Part III--Addendum

236. Aisenberg, Nadya. A Common Spring: Crime Novel
and Classic. Bowling Green, Ohio: Bowling Green University
Popular Press, 1980. 271p. Illus., bibl., index.

Like David Grossvogel in Mystery and Its Fictions (see #44), Aisenberg uses mystery as a jumping-off place for a discussion on general literature. The three writers dealt with in detail as using the ingredients of the mystery for "serious" fictional purposes are Dickens, Conrad, and Greene. A none-too-fresh comparison of the crime novel with myth and the fairy tale is belabored at length in turgid style with much quoting from earlier sources. The detective elements of Hamlet and Oedipus are trotted out once again.

237. Howard, John M. The Movie Murder Mystery Quiz Book. San Diego: Barnes, 1980. 152p. Illus.

Readers steeped in movie mysteries, especially of the thirties and forties, will have a fine time with this collection of topical quizzes, illustrated by black-and-white stills with the answers provided in a separate section in the back.

Part VII--Addendum

CHRISTIE, Agatha

238. Fitzgibbon, Russell H. The Agatha Christie Companion. Bowling Green, Ohio: Bowling Green University Popular Press, 1980. ix, 178p. Bibl., index.

I have seen neither a copy nor a review of this title, but an OCLC entry proves its existence. According to the publisher, it provides a short biography, a summary of critical response, a bibliography, and a character index. In short, everything all the other Christie books put together provide in less than two hundred pages.

239. Toye, Randall. The Agatha Christie Who's Who. New York: Holt, Rinehart, and Winston, 1980. 264p. Illus., bibl., index.

Though I doubt that this biographical dictionary of Christie characters is really necessary, Toye has done the job in excellent fashion. He includes over 2,000 characters, both repeaters (of whom there are a surprising number aside from the famous detectives) and one-shots, chosen for their importance to the plots in which they appear. Murderers are included but not identified as such. Most characters get a one-paragraph identification. Hercule Poirot rates a full page, as does his shadowy brother Achille (about whom Toye has an interesting theory), while Miss Marple and Captain Hastings get about half a page each. Christie is probably the only mystery writer other than Conan Doyle to have a who's-who devoted to her characters.

Toye has done a thorough and admirable job, but there is at least one glaring omission: there is no entry on Mr. Parker Pyne, just a "see" reference to a criminal who once disguised himself as Pyne.

Index references are to entry numbers. The index includes authors, titles, and series included as entries, as well as major subject and author-title references within the annotations. References to titles of entries and names appearing in the headings, as well as authors who are subjects of entire titles in Part VII, have been underlined and appear first. Generally, the following have been omitted from the index: most non-genre-related names, references to misprints and other errors or omissions, cross-references to other works listed in the bibliography, names of newspapers, chapter titles, and references to a character name merely as a means of identifying an author. References to mystery organizations and awards, periodical titles, and well-known essay titles have been included. Book titles appear in all capitals, story and essay titles in quotes. In the case of personal names, no differentiation has been made between actual persons and fictional characters. (Although Rita A. Breen performed most of the labor on this index and is responsible for whatever usefulness it may have, any errors should be blamed on the author.)